M

Terence Rattigan

Born in 1911, a scho[...]ar at Harrow and a[...] Trinity College, Oxford,
Terence Rattigan had [...] his first long[...]running hit in the West End
at the age of twenty-five: *French Without Tears* (1936). His next
play, *After the Da[...]
closed under the g[...]
(1942) Rattigan er[...]

DATE DUE

successes, with m[...]
year and several m[...]
Shines (1943), *Lo[...]
*The Browning Ver[...]
Harlequinade, 194[...]
(1952), *The Sleepi[...]
From the mid-fifti[...]
he enjoyed less su[...]
Praise of Love (19[...]
of his plays turned [...]
of original plays fo[...]
knighted in 1971 a[...]

DEMCO, INC. 38-2931

Terence Rattigan

IN PRAISE
OF LOVE

Introduced by
DAN REBELLATO

London
NICK HERN BOOKS
www.nickhernbooks.demon.co.uk

A Nick Hern Book

This edition of *In Praise of Love* first published as
a paperback original in Great Britain in 2001 by Nick Hem Books,
14 Larden Road, London W3 7ST by arrangement with Methuen.
In Praise of Love was included in *The Collected Plays of Terence
Rattigan* published in 1964 by Hamish Hamilton

Typeset by Country Setting, Kingsdown, Kent CT14 8ES
Printed and bound by Athenaeum Press, Gateshead

A CIP catalogue record for this book is available from
the British Library

ISBN 1 85459 464 8

Terence Rattigan (1911-1977)

Terence Rattigan stood on the steps of the Royal Court Theatre, on 8 May 1956, after the opening night of John Osborne's *Look Back in Anger*. Asked by a reporter what he thought of the play, he replied, with an uncharacteristic lack of discretion, that it should have been retitled 'Look how unlike Terence Rattigan I'm being.' [1] And he was right. The great shifts in British theatre, marked by Osborne's famous première, ushered in kinds of playwriting which were specifically unlike Rattigan's work. The pre-eminence of playwriting as a formal craft, the subtle tracing of the emotional lives of the middle classes – those techniques which Rattigan so perfected – fell dramatically out of favour, creating a veil of prejudice through which his work even now struggles to be seen.

Terence Mervyn Rattigan was born on 10 June 1911, a wet Saturday a few days before George V's coronation. His father, Frank, was in the diplomatic corps and Terry's parents were often posted abroad, leaving him to be raised by his paternal grandmother. Frank Rattigan was a geographically and emotionally distant man, who pursued a string of little-disguised affairs throughout his marriage. Rattigan would later draw on these memories when he created Mark St Neots, the bourgeois Casanova of *Who is Sylvia?* Rattigan was much closer to his mother, Vera Rattigan, and they remained close friends until her death in 1971.

Rattigan's parents were not great theatregoers, but Frank Rattigan's brother had married a Gaiety Girl, causing a minor family uproar, and an apocryphal story suggests that the 'indulgent aunt' reported as taking the young Rattigan to the theatre may have been this scandalous relation.[2] And when, in the summer of 1922, his family went to stay in the country cottage of the drama critic Hubert Griffiths, Rattigan avidly worked through his extensive library of playscripts. Terry went to Harrow in 1925, and there maintained both his somewhat illicit theatregoing habit and his insatiable reading, reputedly devouring every play in the school library. Apart from contemporary authors like Galsworthy, Shaw and Barrie, he also read the plays of Chekhov, a writer whose crucial influence he often acknowledged.[3]

His early attempts at writing, while giving little sign of his later sophistication, do indicate his ability to absorb and reproduce his own theatrical experiences. There was a ten-minute melodrama

about the Borgias entitled *The Parchment*, on the cover of which
the author recommends with admirable conviction that a suitable
cast for this work might comprise 'Godfrey Tearle, Gladys
Cooper, Marie Tempest, Matheson Lang, Isobel Elsom, Henry
Ainley . . . [and] Noël Coward'.[4] At Harrow, when one of his
teachers demanded a French playlet for a composition exercise,
Rattigan, undaunted by his linguistic shortcomings, produced a
full-throated tragedy of deception, passion and revenge which
included the immortal curtain line: 'COMTESSE. (*Souffrant
terriblement.*) Non! non! non! Ah non! Mon Dieu, non!' [5] His
teacher's now famous response was 'French execrable: theatre
sense first class'.[6] A year later, aged fifteen, he wrote *The Pure in
Heart,* a rather more substantial play showing a family being
pulled apart by a son's crime and the father's desire to maintain
his reputation. Rattigan's ambitions were plainly indicated on the
title pages, each of which announced the author to be 'the famous
playwrite and author T. M. Rattigan.' [7]

Frank Rattigan was less than keen on having a 'playwrite' for a
son and was greatly relieved when in 1930, paving the way for a
life as a diplomat, Rattigan gained a scholarship to read History at
Trinity, Oxford. But Rattigan's interests were entirely elsewhere.
A burgeoning political conscience that had led him to oppose the
compulsory Officer Training Corps parades at Harrow saw him
voice pacifist and socialist arguments at college, even supporting
the controversial Oxford Union motion 'This House will in no
circumstances fight for its King and Country' in February 1933.
The rise of Hitler (which he briefly saw close at hand when he
spent some weeks in the Black Forest in July 1933) and the
outbreak of the Spanish Civil War saw his radical leanings deepen
and intensify. Rattigan never lost his political compassion. After
the war he drifted towards the Liberal Party, but he always insisted
that he had never voted Conservative, despite the later conception
of him as a Tory playwright of the establishment.[8]

Away from the troubled atmosphere of his family, Rattigan
began to gain in confidence as the contours of his ambitions and
his identity moved more sharply into focus. He soon took
advantage of the university's theatrical facilities and traditions.
He joined The Oxford Union Dramatic Society (OUDS), where
contemporaries included Giles Playfair, George Devine, Peter
Glenville, Angus Wilson and Frith Banbury. Each year, OUDS ran
a one-act play competition and in Autumn 1931 Rattigan
submitted one. Unusually, it seems that this was a highly experimental effort, somewhat like Konstantin's piece in *The Seagull.*
George Devine, the OUDS president, apparently told the young
author, 'Some of it is absolutely smashing, but it goes too far'. [9]
Rattigan was instead to make his first mark as a somewhat
scornful reviewer for the student newspaper, *Cherwell,* and as a

performer in the Smokers (OUDS's private revue club), where he
adopted the persona and dress of 'Lady Diana Coutigan', a drag
performance which allowed him to discuss leading members of the
Society with a barbed camp wit.[10]

That the name of his Smokers persona echoed the contemporary
phrase, 'queer as a coot', indicates Rattigan's new-found
confidence in his homosexuality. In February 1932, Rattigan
played a tiny part in the OUDS production of *Romeo and Juliet*,
which was directed by John Gielgud and starred Peggy Ashcroft
and Edith Evans (women undergraduates were not admitted to
OUDS, and professional actresses were often recruited).
Rattigan's failure to deliver his one line correctly raised an
increasingly embarrassing laugh every night (an episode which he
re-uses to great effect in *Harlequinade*). However, out of this
production came a friendship with Gielgud and his partner, John
Perry. Through them, Rattigan was introduced to theatrical and
homosexual circles, where his youthful 'school captain' looks
were much admired.

A growing confidence in his sexuality and in his writing led to his
first major play. In 1931, he shared rooms with a contemporary of
his, Philip Heimann, who was having an affair with Irina
Basilevich, a mature student. Rattigan's own feelings for Heimann
completed an eternal triangle that formed the basis of the play he
co-wrote with Heimann, *First Episode*. This play was accepted for
production in Surrey's "Q" theatre; it was respectfully received and
subsequently transferred to the Comedy Theatre in London's West
End, though carefully shorn of its homosexual subplot. Despite
receiving only £50 from this production (and having put £200 into
it), Rattigan immediately dropped out of college to become a full-
time writer.

Frank Rattigan was displeased by this move, but made a deal with
his son. He would give him an allowance of £200 a year for two
years and let him live at home to write; if at the end of that period,
he had had no discernible success, he would enter a more secure
and respectable profession. With this looming deadline, Rattigan
wrote quickly. *Black Forest*, an O'Neill-inspired play based on his
experiences in Germany in 1933, is one of the three that have
survived. Rather unwillingly, he collaborated with Hector Bolitho
on an adaptation of the latter's novel, *Grey Farm*, which received a
disastrous New York production in 1940. Another project was an
adaptation of *A Tale of Two Cities*, written with Gielgud; this
fell through at the last minute when Donald Albery, the play's
potential producer, received a complaint from actor-manager
John Martin-Harvey who was beginning a farewell tour of his
own adaptation, *The Only Way*, which he had been performing for
forty-five years. As minor compensation, Albery invited Rattigan
to send him any other new scripts. Rattigan sent him a play pro-

visionally titled *Gone Away*, based on his experiences in a French language Summer School in 1931. Albery took out a nine-month option on it, but no production appeared.

By mid-1936, Rattigan was despairing. His father had secured him a job with Warner Brothers as an in-house screenwriter, which was reasonably paid; but Rattigan wanted success in the theatre, and his desk-bound life at Teddington Studios seemed unlikely to advance this ambition. By chance, one of Albery's productions was unexpectedly losing money, and the wisest course of action seemed to be to pull the show and replace it with something cheap. Since *Gone Away* required a relatively small cast and only one set, Albery quickly arranged for a production. Harold French, the play's director, had only one qualm: the title. Rattigan suggested *French Without Tears*, which was immediately adopted.

After an appalling dress rehearsal, no one anticipated the rapturous response of the first-night audience, led by Cicely Courtneidge's infectious laugh. The following morning Kay Hammond, the show's female lead, discovered Rattigan surrounded by the next day's reviews. 'But I don't believe it', he said. 'Even *The Times* likes it.' [11]

French Without Tears played over 1000 performances in its three-year run and Rattigan was soon earning £100 a week. He moved out of his father's home, wriggled out of his Warner Brothers contract, and dedicated himself to spending the money as soon as it came in. Partly this was an attempt to defer the moment when he had to follow up this enormous success. In the event, both of his next plays were undermined by the outbreak of war.

After the Dance, an altogether more bleak indictment of the Bright Young Things' failure to engage with the iniquities and miseries of contemporary life, opened, in June 1939, to euphoric reviews; but only a month later the European crisis was darkening the national mood and audiences began to dwindle. The play was pulled in August after only sixty performances. *Follow My Leader* was a satirical farce closely based on the rise of Hitler, co-written with an Oxford contemporary, Tony Goldschmidt (writing as Anthony Maurice in case anyone thought he was German). It suffered an alternative fate. Banned from production in 1938, owing to the Foreign Office's belief that 'the production of this play at this time would not be in the best interests of the country',[12] it finally received its première in 1940, by which time Rattigan and Goldschmidt's mild satire failed to capture the real fears that the war was unleashing in the country.

Rattigan's insecurity about writing now deepened. An interest in Freud, dating back to his Harrow days, encouraged him to visit a psychiatrist that he had known while at Oxford, Dr Keith Newman. Newman exerted a svengali-like influence on Rattigan and persuaded the pacifist playwright to join the RAF as a means of curing his writer's block. Oddly, this unorthodox treatment seemed to have some effect; by 1941, Rattigan was writing again. On one dramatic sea crossing, an engine failed, and with everyone forced to jettison all excess baggage and possessions, Rattigan threw the hard covers and blank pages from the notebook containing his new play, stuffing the precious manuscript into his jacket.

Rattigan drew on his RAF experiences to write a new play, *Flare Path*. Bronson Albery and Bill Linnit who had both supported *French Without Tears* both turned the play down, believing that the last thing that the public wanted was a play about the war.[13] H. M. Tennent Ltd., led by the elegant Hugh 'Binkie' Beaumont, was the third management offered the script; and in 1942, *Flare Path* opened in London, eventually playing almost 700 performances. Meticulously interweaving the stories of three couples against the backdrop of wartime uncertainty, Rattigan found himself 'commended, if not exactly as a professional playwright, at least as a promising apprentice who had definitely begun to learn the rudiments of his job'.[14] Beaumont, already on the way to becoming the most powerful and successful West End producer of the era, was an influential ally for Rattigan. There is a curious side-story to this production; Dr Keith Newman decided to watch 250 performances of this play and write up the insights that his 'serial attendance' had afforded him. George Bernard Shaw remarked that such playgoing behaviour 'would have driven me mad; and I am not sure that [Newman] came out of it without a slight derangement'. Shaw's caution was wise.[15] In late 1945, Newman went insane and eventually died in a psychiatric hospital.

Meanwhile, Rattigan had achieved two more successes; the witty farce, *While the Sun Shines*, and the more serious, though politically clumsy, *Love in Idleness* (retitled *O Mistress Mine* in America). He had also co-written a number of successful films, including *The Day Will Dawn, Uncensored, The Way to the Stars* and an adaptation of *French Without Tears*. By the end of 1944, Rattigan had three plays running in the West End, a record only beaten by Somerset Maugham's four in 1908.

Love in Idleness was dedicated to Henry 'Chips' Channon, the Tory MP who had become Rattigan's lover. Channon's otherwise gossipy diaries record their meeting very discreetly: 'I dined with Juliet Duff in her little flat . . . also there, Sibyl Colefax and Master Terence Rattigan, and we sparkled over the Burgundy. I like Rattigan enormously, and feel a new friendship has begun. He has a flat in Albany'.[16] Tom Driberg's rather less discreet account fleshes out the story: Channon's 'seduction of the playwright was almost like the wooing of Danaë by Zeus – every day the playwright found, delivered to his door, a splendid present – a case of champagne, a huge pot of caviar, a Cartier cigarette-box in two kinds of gold . . . In the end, of course, he gave in, saying apologetically to his friends, "How can one *not?*" '.[17] It was a very different set in which Rattigan now moved, one that was wealthy and conservative, the very people he had criticised in *After the Dance*. Rattigan did not share the complacency of many of his friends, and his next play revealed a deepening complexity and ambition.

For a long time, Rattigan had nurtured a desire to become respected as a serious writer; the commercial success of *French Without Tears* had, however, sustained the public image of Rattigan as a wealthy young light comedy writer-about-town. [18] With *The Winslow Boy*, which premièred in 1946, Rattigan began to turn this image around. In doing so he entered a new phase as a playwright. As one contemporary critic observed, this play 'put him at once into the class of the serious and distinguished writer'.[19] The play, based on the Archer-Shee case in which a family attempted to sue the Admiralty for a false accusation of theft against their son, featured some of Rattigan's most elegantly crafted and subtle characterization yet. The famous second curtain, when the barrister Robert Morton subjects Ronnie Winslow to a vicious interrogation before announcing that 'The boy is plainly innocent. I accept the brief', brought a joyous standing ovation on the first night. No less impressive is the subtle handling of the concept of 'justice' and 'rights' through the play of ironies which pits Morton's liberal complacency against Catherine Winslow's feminist convictions.

Two years later, Rattigan's *Playbill*, comprising the one-act plays *The Browning Version* and *Harlequinade*, showed an ever deepening talent. The latter is a witty satire of the kind of touring theatre encouraged by the new Committee for the Encouragement of Music and Arts (CEMA, the immediate forerunner of the Arts Council). But the former's depiction of a failed, repressed Classics teacher evinced an ability to choreograph emotional subtleties on stage that outstripped anything Rattigan had yet demonstrated.

Adventure Story, which in 1949 followed hard on the heels of *Playbill*, was less successful. An attempt to dramatize the emotional dilemmas of Alexander the Great, Rattigan seemed unable to escape the vernacular of his own circle, and the epic scheme of the play sat oddly with Alexander's more prosaic concerns.

Rattigan's response to both the critical bludgeoning of this play and the distinctly luke-warm reception of *Playbill* on Broadway was to write a somewhat extravagant article for the *New Statesman*. 'Concerning the Play of Ideas' was a desire to defend the place of 'character' against those who would insist on the pre-

eminence in drama of ideas.[20] The essay is not clear and is
couched in such teasing terms that it is at first difficult to see why
it should have secured such a fervent response. James Bridie,
Benn Levy, Peter Ustinov, Sean O'Casey, Ted Willis, Christopher
Fry and finally George Bernard Shaw all weighed in to support or
condemn the article. Finally Rattigan replied in slightly more
moderate terms to these criticisms insisting (and the first essay
reasonably supports this) that he was not calling for the end of
ideas in the theatre, but rather their inflection through character
and situation.[21] However, the damage was done (as, two years
later, with his 'Aunt Edna', it would again be done). Rattigan was
increasingly being seen as the arch-proponent of commercial
vacuity.[22]

The play Rattigan had running at the time added weight to his
opponents' charge. Originally planned as a dark comedy, *Who is
Sylvia?* became a rather more frivolous thing both in the writing
and the playing. Rattled by the failure of *Adventure Story*, and
superstitiously aware that the new play was opening at the
Criterion, where fourteen years before *French Without Tears* had
been so successful, Rattigan and everyone involved in the
production had steered it towards light farce and obliterated the
residual seriousness of the original conceit.

Rattigan had ended his affair with Henry Channon and again taken
up with Kenneth Morgan, a young actor who had appeared in
Follow My Leader and the film of *French Without Tears*. However,
the relationship had not lasted and Morgan had for a while been
seeing someone else. Rattigan's distress was compounded one day
in February 1949, when he received a message that Morgan had
killed himself. Although horrified, Rattigan soon began to
conceive an idea for a play. The result is one of the finest
examples of Rattigan's craft. The story of Hester Collyer, trapped
in a relationship with a man incapable of returning her love, and
her transition from attempted suicide to groping, uncertain self-
determination is handled with extraordinary economy, precision
and power. The depths of despair and desire that Rattigan plumbs
have made *The Deep Blue Sea* one of his most popular and
moving pieces.

1953 saw Rattigan's romantic comedy *The Sleeping Prince*, planned
as a modest, if belated, contribution to the Coronation festivities.
However, the project was hypertrophied by the insistent presence of
Laurence Olivier and Vivien Leigh in the cast and the critics were
disturbed to see such whimsy from the author of *The Deep Blue Sea*.

Two weeks after its opening, the first two volumes of Rattigan's
Collected Plays were published. The preface to the second volume
introduced one of Rattigan's best-known, and most notorious
creations: Aunt Edna. 'Let us invent,' he writes, 'a character, a

nice respectable, middle-class, middle-aged, maiden lady, with time on her hands and the money to help her pass it'.[23] Rattigan paints a picture of this eternal theatregoer, whose bewildered disdain for modernism ('Picasso – "those dreadful reds, my dear, and why three noses?" ')[24] make up part of the particular challenge of dramatic writing. The intertwined commercial and cultural pressures that the audience brings with it exert considerable force on the playwright's work.

Rattigan's creation brought considerable scorn upon his head. But Rattigan is neither patronizing nor genuflecting towards Aunt Edna. The whole essay is aimed at demonstrating the crucial rôle of the audience in the theatrical experience. Rattigan's own sense of theatre was *learned* as a member of the audience, and he refuses to distance himself from this woman: 'despite my already self-acknowledged creative ambitions I did not in the least feel myself a being apart. If my neighbours gasped with fear for the heroine when she was confronted with a fate worse than death, I gasped with them'.[25] But equally, he sees his job as a writer to engage in a gentle tug-of-war with the audience's expectations: 'although Aunt Edna must never be made mock of, or bored, or befuddled, she must equally not be wooed, or pandered to or cosseted'.[26] The complicated relation between satisfying and surprising this figure may seem contradictory, but as Rattigan notes, 'Aunt Edna herself is indeed a highly contradictory character'.[27]

But Rattigan's argument, as in the 'Play of Ideas' debate before it, was taken to imply an insipid pandering to the unchallenging expectations of his audience. Aunt Edna dogged his career from that moment on and she became such a by-word for what theatre should *not* be that in 1960, the Questors Theatre, Ealing, could title a triple-bill of Absurdist plays, 'Not For Aunt Edna'.[28]

Rattigan's next play did help to restore his reputation as a serious dramatist. *Separate Tables* was another double-bill, set in a small Bournemouth hotel. The first play develops Rattigan's familiar themes of sexual longing and humiliation while the second pits a man found guilty of interfering with women in a local cinema against the self-appointed moral jurors in the hotel. The evening was highly acclaimed and the subsequent Broadway production a rare American success.

However, Rattigan's reign as the leading British playwright was about to be brought to an abrupt end. In a car from Stratford to London, early in 1956, Rattigan spent two and a half hours informing his Oxford contemporary George Devine why the new play he had discovered would not work in the theatre. When Devine persisted, Rattigan answered 'Then I know nothing about plays'. To which Devine replied, 'You know everything about plays, but you don't know a fucking thing about *Look Back in Anger.*' [29] Rattigan only barely attended the first night. He and Hugh Beaumont wanted to leave at the interval until the critic T. C. Worsley persuaded them to stay.[30]

The support for the English Stage Company's initiative was soon overwhelming. Osborne's play was acclaimed by the influential critics Kenneth Tynan and Harold Hobson, and the production was revived frequently at the Court, soon standing as the banner under which that disparate band of men (and women), the Angry Young Men, would assemble. Like many of his contemporaries, Rattigan decried the new movements, Beckett and Ionesco's turn from Naturalism, the wild invective of Osborne, the passionate socialism of Wesker, the increasing influence of Brecht. His opposition to them was perhaps intemperate, but he knew what was at stake: 'I may be prejudiced, but I'm pretty sure it won't survive,' he said in 1960, 'I'm prejudiced because if it *does* survive, I know I won't.' [31]

Such was the power and influence of the new movement that Rattigan almost immediately seemed old-fashioned. And from now on, his plays began to receive an almost automatic panning. His first play since *Separate Tables* (1954) was *Variation on a Theme* (1958). But between those dates the critical mood had changed. To make matters worse, there was the widely publicized story that nineteen year-old Shelagh Delaney had written the successful *A Taste of Honey* in two weeks after having seen *Variation on a Theme* and deciding that she could do better. A more sinister aspect of the response was the increasingly open accusation that Rattigan was dishonestly concealing a covert homosexual play within an apparently heterosexual one. The two champions of Osborne's play, Tynan and Hobson, were joined by Gerard Fay in the *Manchester Guardian* and Alan Brien in the *Spectator* to ask 'Are Things What They Seem?' [32]

When he is not being attacked for smuggling furtively homosexual themes into apparently straight plays, Rattigan is also criticized for lacking the courage to 'come clean' about his sexuality, both in his life and in his writing.[33] But neither of these criticisms really hit the mark. On the one hand, it is rather disingenuous to suggest that Rattigan should have 'come out'. The 1950s were a difficult time for homosexual men. The flight to the Soviet Union of Burgess and Maclean in 1951 sparked off a major witch-hunt against homosexuals, especially those in prominent positions. Cecil Beaton and Benjamin Britten were rumoured to be targets.[34] The police greatly stepped up the investigation and entrapment of homosexuals and prosecutions rose dramatically at the end of the forties, reaching a peak in 1953-54. One of their most infamous arrests for importuning, in October 1953, was that of John Gielgud.[35]

But neither is it quite correct to imply that somehow Rattigan's plays are *really* homosexual. This would be to misunderstand the way that homosexuality figured in the forties and early fifties. Wartime London saw a considerable expansion in the number of pubs and bars where homosexual men (and women) could meet. This network sustained a highly sophisticated system of gestural and dress codes, words and phrases that could be used to indicate one's sexual desires, many of them drawn from theatrical slang. But the illegality of any homosexual activity ensured that these codes could never become *too* explicit, *too* clear. Homosexuality, then, was explored and experienced through a series of semi-hidden, semi-open codes of behaviour; the image of the iceberg, with the greater part of its bulk submerged beneath the surface, was frequently employed.[36] And this image is, of course, one of the metaphors often used to describe Rattigan's own playwriting.

Reaction came in the form of a widespread paranoia about the apparent increase in homosexuality. The fifties saw a major drive to seek out, understand, and often 'cure' homosexuality. The impetus of these investigations was to bring the unspeakable and underground activities of, famously, 'Evil Men' into the open, to make it fully visible. The Wolfenden Report of 1957 was, without doubt, a certain kind of liberalizing document in its recommendation that consensual sex between adult men in private be legalized. However the other side of its effect is to reinstate the integrity of those boundaries – private/public, hidden/exposed, homosexual/heterosexual – which homosexuality was broaching. The criticisms of Rattigan are precisely part of this same desire to divide, clarify and expose.

Many of Rattigan's plays were originally conceived with homosexual characters (*French Without Tears*, *The Deep Blue Sea* and *Separate Tables*, for example), which he then changed.[37] But many more of them hint at homosexual experiences and activities: the relationship between Tony and David in *First Episode*, the Major in *Follow my Leader* who is blackmailed over an incident in Baghdad ('After all,' he explains, 'a chap's only human, and it was a deuced hot night –'),[38] the suspiciously polymorphous servicemen of *While the Sun Shines*, Alexander the Great and T. E. Lawrence from *Adventure Story* and *Ross*, Mr Miller in *The Deep Blue Sea* and several others. Furthermore, rumours of Rattigan's own bachelor life circulated fairly widely. As indicated above, Rattigan always placed great trust in the audiences of his plays, and it was the audience which had to decode and reinterpret these plays. His plays cannot be judged by the criterion of 'honesty' and 'explicitness' that obsessed a generation after Osborne. They are plays which negotiate sexual desire through structures of hint, implications and metaphor. As David Rudkin has suggested, 'the craftsmanship of which we hear so much loose talk seems to me to arise from deep psychological necessity, a drive to organize the energy that arises out of his own pain. Not to batten it down but to invest it with some expressive clarity that speaks immediately to people, yet keeps itself hidden'.[39]

The shifts in the dominant view of both homosexuality and the theatre that took place in the fifties account for the brutal decline of Rattigan's career. He continued writing, and while *Ross* (1960) was reasonably well received, his ill-judged musical adaptation of *French Without Tears, Joie de Vivre* (1960), was a complete disaster, not assisted by a liberal bout of laryngitis among the cast, and the unexpected insanity of the pianist.[40] It ran for four performances.

During the sixties, Rattigan was himself dogged with ill-health: pneumonia and hepatitis were followed by leukaemia. When his death conspicuously failed to transpire, this last diagnosis was admitted to be incorrect. Despite this, he continued to write, producing the successful television play *Heart to Heart* in 1962, and the stage play *Man and Boy* the following year, which received the same sniping that greeted *Variation on a Theme*. In 1964, he wrote *Nelson – a Portrait in Miniature* for Associated Television, as part of a short season of his plays.

It was at this point that Rattigan decided to leave Britain and live abroad. Partly this decision was taken for reasons of health; but partly Rattigan just seemed no longer to be welcome. Ironically, it was the same charge being levelled at Rattigan that he had faced in the thirties, when the newspapers thundered against the those who had supported the Oxford Union's pacifist motion as 'woolly-minded Communists, practical jokers and sexual indeterminates'.[41] As he confessed in an interview late in his life, 'Overnight almost, we were told we were old-fashioned and effete and corrupt and finished, and . . . I somehow accepted Tynan's verdict and went off to Hollywood to write film scripts'.[42] In 1967 he moved to Bermuda as a tax exile. A stage adaptation of his Nelson play, as *Bequest to the Nation*, had a luke-warm reception.

Rattigan had a bad sixties, but his seventies seemed to indicate a turnaround in his fortunes and reputation. At the end of 1970, a successful production of *The Winslow Boy* was the first of ten years of acclaimed revivals. In 1972, Hampstead Theatre revived *While the Sun Shines* and a year later the Young Vic was praised for its *French Without Tears*. In 1976 and 1977 *The Browning Version* was revived at the King's Head and *Separate Tables* at the Apollo. Rattigan briefly returned to Britain in 1971, pulled partly by his renewed fortune and partly by the fact that he was given a knighthood in the New Year's honours list. Another double bill followed in 1973: *In Praise of Love* comprised the weak *Before Dawn* and the moving tale of emotional concealment and creativity, *After Lydia*. Critical reception was more respectful than usual, although the throwaway farce of the first play detracted from the quality of the second.

Cause Célèbre, commissioned by BBC Radio and others, concerned the Rattenbury case, in which Alma Rattenbury's aged husband was beaten to death by her eighteen year-old lover. Shortly after its radio première, Rattigan was diagnosed with bone cancer. Rattigan's response, having been through the false leukaemia scare in the early sixties, was to greet the news with unruffled elegance, welcoming the opportunity to 'work harder and indulge myself more'.[43] The hard work included a play about the Asquith family and a stage adaptation of *Cause Célèbre*, but, as production difficulties began to arise over the latter, the Asquith play slipped out of Rattigan's grasp. Although very ill, he returned to Britain, and on 4 July 1977, he was taken by limousine from his hospital bed to Her Majesty's Theatre, where he watched his last ever première. A fortnight later he had a car drive him around the West End where two of his plays were then running before boarding the plane for the last time. On 30 November 1977, in Bermuda, he died.

As Michael Billington's perceptive obituary noted, 'his whole work is a sustained assault on English middle class values: fear of emotional commitment, terror in the face of passion, apprehension about sex'.[44] In death, Rattigan began once again to be seen as someone critically opposed to the values with which he had so long been associated, a writer dramatizing dark moments of bleak compassion and aching desire.

Notes

1. Quoted in Rattigan's *Daily Telegraph* obituary (1 December 1977).

2. Michael Darlow and Gillian Hodson. *Terence Rattigan: The Man and His Work*. London and New York: Quartet Books, 1979, p. 26.

3. See, for example, Sheridan Morley. 'Terence Rattigan at 65.' *The Times*. (9 May 1977).

4. Terence Rattigan. Preface. *The Collected Plays of Terence Rattigan: Volume Two*. London: Hamish Hamilton, 1953, p. xv.

5. *Ibid.*, p. viii.

6. *Ibid.*, p. vii.

7. *Ibid.*, p. vii.

8. cf. Sheridan Morley, *op. cit.*

9. Humphrey Carpenter. *OUDS: A Centenary History of the Oxford University Dramatic Society*. With a Prologue by Robert Robinson. Oxford: Oxford University Press, 1985, p. 123.

10. Rattigan may well have reprised this later in life. John Osborne, in his autobiography, recalls a friend showing him a picture of Rattigan performing in an RAF drag show: 'He showed me a photograph of himself with Rattigan, dressed in a *tutu*, carrying a wand, accompanied by a line of aircraftsmen, during which Terry had sung his own show-stopper, "I'm just about the oldest

fairy in the business. I'm quite the oldest fairy that you've ever seen".' John Osborne. *A Better Class of Person: An Autobiography, Volume I 1929-1956.* London: Faber and Faber, 1981, p. 223.

11. Darlow and Hodson *op. cit.*, p. 83.

12. Norman Gwatkin. Letter to Gilbert Miller, 28 July 1938. in: *Follow My Leader.* Lord Chamberlain's Correspondence: LR 1938. [British Library].

13. Richard Huggett. *Binkie Beaumont: Eminence Grise of the West Theatre 1933-1973.* London: Hodder & Stoughton, 1989, p. 308.

14. Terence Rattigan. Preface. *The Collected Plays of Terence Rattigan: Volume One.* London: Hamish Hamilton, 1953, p. xiv.

15. George Bernard Shaw, in: Keith Newman. *Two Hundred and Fifty Times I Saw a Play: or, Authors, Actors and Audiences.* With the facsimile of a comment by Bernard Shaw. Oxford: Pelagos Press, 1944, p. 2.

16. Henry Channon. *Chips: The Diaries of Sir Henry Channon.* Edited by Robert Rhodes James. Harmondsworth: Penguin, 1974, p. 480. Entry for 29 September 1944.

17. Tom Driberg. *Ruling Passions.* London: Jonathan Cape, 1977, p. 186.

18. See, for example, Norman Hart. 'Introducing Terence Rattigan,' *Theatre World.* xxxi, 171. (April 1939). p. 180 or Ruth Jordan. 'Another Adventure Story,' *Woman's Journal.* (August 1949), pp. 31-32.

19. Audrey Williamson. *Theatre of Two Decades.* New York and London: Macmillan, 1951, p. 100.

20. Terence Rattigan. 'Concerning the Play of Ideas,' *New Statesman and Nation.* (4 March 1950), pp. 241-242.

21. Terence Rattigan. 'The Play of Ideas,' *New Statesman and Nation.* (13 May 1950), pp. 545-546. See also Susan Rusinko, 'Rattigan versus Shaw: The 'Drama of Ideas' Debate'. in: *Shaw: The Annual of Bernard Shaw Studies: Volume Two.* Edited by Stanley Weintraub. University Park, Penn: Pennsylvania State University Press, 1982. pp. 171-78.

22. John Elsom writes that Rattigan's plays 'represented establishment writing'. *Post-War British Drama.* Revised Edition. London: Routledge, 1979, p. 33.

23. Terence Rattigan. *Coll. Plays: Vol. Two. op. cit.*, pp. xi-xii.

24. *Ibid.,* p. xii.

25. *Ibid.,* p. xiv.

26. *Ibid.,* p. xvi.

27. *Ibid.,* p. xviii.

28. Opened on 17 September 1960. cf. *Plays and Players.* vii, 11 (November 1960).

29. Quoted in Irving Wardle. *The Theatres of George Devine.* London: Jonathan Cape, 1978, p. 180.

30. John Osborne. *Almost a Gentleman: An Autobiography, Volume II 1955-1966.* London: Faber and Faber, 1991, p. 20.

31. Robert Muller. 'Soul-Searching with Terence Rattigan.' *Daily Mail.* (30 April 1960).

32. The headline of Hobson's review in the *Sunday Times,* 11 May 1958.

33. See, for example, Nicholas de Jongh. *Not in Front of the Audience: Homosexuality on Stage.* London: Routledge, 1992, pp. 55-58.

34. Kathleen Tynan. *The Life of Kenneth Tynan.* Corrected Edition. London: Methuen, 1988, p. 118.

35. Cf. Jeffrey Weeks. *Coming Out: Homosexual Politics in Britain from the Nineteenth Century to the Present.* Revised and Updated Edition. London and New York: Quartet, 1990, p. 58; Peter Wildeblood. *Against the Law.*

London: Weidenfeld and Nicolson, 1955, p. 46. The story of Gielgud's arrest may be found in Huggett, *op. cit.,* pp. 429-431. It was Gielgud's arrest which apparently inspired Rattigan to write the second part of *Separate Tables,* although again, thanks this time to the Lord Chamberlain, Rattigan had to change the Major's offence to a heterosexual one. See Darlow and Hodson, *op. cit.,* p. 228.

36. See, for example, Rodney Garland's novel about homosexual life in London, *The Heart in Exile.* London: W. H. Allen, 1953, p. 104.

37. See note 36; and also 'Rattigan Talks to John Simon,' *Theatre Arts.* 46 (April 1962), p. 24.

38. Terence Rattigan and Anthony Maurice. *Follow my Leader.* Typescript. Lord Chamberlain Play Collection: 1940/2. Box 2506. [British Library].

39. Quoted in Darlow and Hodson, *op. cit.,* p. 15.

40. B. A. Young, *op. cit.,* p. 162.

41. Quoted in Darlow and Hodson, *op. cit.,* p. 56.

42. Quoted in Sheridan Morley, *op. cit.*

43. Darlow and Hodson, *op. cit.,* p. 308.

44. *Guardian.* (2 December 1977).

In Praise of Love

In Praise of Love, opened on 27 September 1973 at the Duchess Theatre, in the West End of London where, twenty-one years earlier, *The Deep Blue Sea* had been one of Terence Rattigan's greatest critical and commercial successes. But by the early seventies, the prospect of a new Rattigan play did not seem to quicken the theatregoer's heart, and if Rattigan had hoped to repeat the triumph of *The Deep Blue Sea*, he was to be disappointed.

A new generation of critics had been reared on the attitude and example of Kenneth Tynan, the champion of the New Wave, that outpouring of socially committed, theatrically experimental theatre workers which followed in the wake of John Osborne's *Look Back in Anger* (1956). J. C. Trewin, a survivor from an era more attuned to Rattigan's project, found in the new play 'moments of agonized realization that I have found shattering: none can belittle such work as this'. Unfortunately, most of the critics were going to try. B. A. Young, critic of the *Financial Times* and long-time supporter and friend of Rattigan, was on holiday, and his place was filled by a young second-stringer, Michael Coveney. The resulting notice was withering in its contempt for this 'witless junk paraded under the banner of a reputation'. In the *Guardian* Michael Billington, another critic who had learned his trade by the light of Tynan's fiery certainty, saw it as 'a rather crude and obvious piece of audience-manipulation'. Milton Shulman in the *Evening Standard* suspected it to be 'only a tear-jerker masquerading as a significant dramatic statement'.[1]

This was not, however, the universal view. One critic in particular was determined to buck the theatrical trend. Harold Hobson, having survived the sweeping theatrical changes of the fifties, and indeed personal attacks on him by Tynan's supporters,[2] rebuked his colleagues in a review which declared

> This is a play of unostentatious courage that requires courage to watch. Plainly it has frightened one of my tougher colleagues out of his wits, brutality being a sure sign of panic: but to others, whatever courage is involved will be abundantly rewarded. Rattigan has never written better than this: and in this form of drama no one has ever written better than Rattigan [. . .] [*In Praise of Love*] is the most piercing exposition of love under great stress that I have ever seen on the stage; it is an experience of such power and beauty as will intensify one's appreciation of what consummate theatre can achieve.[3]

But even Hobson's endorsement could not help the play. The Duchess is a small theatre with a capacity of less than 500, so its run of a little over four months was another blow to Rattigan. While plays like *Separate Tables, The Winslow Boy, The Browning Version* and *The Deep Blue Sea* have regained a firm place in the history of twentieth-century theatre, his later – post-Osborne – plays have fared less well. Although reviewers of recent revivals have tended to side more with Hobson than Coveney, *In Praise of Love* is still sometimes misrecognised as sentimental, formally conservative, and emotionally destitute.

The play is set in a small flat in Islington, the home of Sebastian and Lydia Cruttwell. Sebastian was a once-promising novelist, now a critic with Marxist sympathies. His sardonic indifference is tolerated amicably by Lydia, an Estonian refugee, whom Sebastian married after the war to secure her a British passport, and whom he seems absent-mindedly to have neglected to divorce ever since. But Lydia is dying: she has been diagnosed with advanced poly-arteritis, and, despite her doctor's encouraging and false medical reports, she has discovered that she is unlikely to live more than a year. She confides all this to a family friend, Mark Walters, but, wanting to spare him anxiety, not to Sebastian. When Sebastian fails to appear to watch a television play written by their son, Joey, this particularly enrages Lydia, who had just managed to secure a precarious *rapprochement* between negligent father and resentful son. Sebastian is forced to admit to Mark that he knows all about the illness, and has been keeping Lydia in a state of what he believes to be sublime ignorance. Being told the diagnosis has made Sebastian realise how much he loves his wife, though the need to persuade her that everything is normal has forced him painfully to continue a subterfuge of cantankerous off-handedness. Mark, caught between the loyalties of his old friend and the woman he has always loved, points Lydia towards the truth. Lydia, astonished by the revelation that Sebastian knows, and by the implication that he loves her, leaves Sebastian and Joey to work through their differences over a game of chess.

In its meticulous interweaving of white lies, painful deceptions, and compassionate untruth, the play is, as Geoffrey Wansell has written, Rattigan's 'own obituary; his apologia for his own life'.[4] There are, as we shall see, distant echoes of Rattigan's own experience at every level of this complex and moving work. But there is a more direct source for the play which dates back to 1957 and Rattigan's friendship with Rex Harrison and his wife, Kay Kendall, a young actress who had made a considerable impact with her delightful performance in the British film comedy *Genevieve* (1953).

Harrison had met Kendall in the spring of 1954. Although married to his second wife, Lilli Palmer, Harrison began an affair with Kendall which, by the summer of 1956, had become more serious than either of them had expected. Harrison had scored his first major success in the premiere of *French Without Tears* twenty years earlier and in the summer of 1957 Rattigan stayed with the couple in Beverly Hills (in a house they shared with Gladys Cooper's dog, June). Harrison was on a break from performing in *My Fair Lady* on Broadway, Kendall was making *Les Girls* in Hollywood, and Rattigan was working on his screenplay for *Separate Tables*.[5] Knowing the depth of his old friend's feelings, Rattigan was surprised by the coldness with which Harrison treated Kendall. But it was only at the end of that year, when Rattigan joined them again in St Moritz that Harrison explained the situation.

Throughout 1956, Kendall had been suffering from profound bouts of fatigue; in early January 1957, Harrison was summoned by her doctor, who informed him that she had myeloid leukaemia, and that 'there is nothing to be done'.[6] The doctor had curiously chosen not to inform his patient and instead left it to Harrison to decide what to do. Rather than reveal to Kendall that she had a couple of years to live, Harrison persuaded her that she had anaemia, insisting on the story even when an Italian magazine reported her true diagnosis. He explained the situation to his wife, Lilli Palmer, who agreed to a divorce so that he could marry Kendall, which he did in June 1957. What is more, a notoriously irascible man, Harrison felt that maintaining the facade of normality required him to hide his concern under a mask of indifference and rudeness at all times: this was the root of the behaviour Rattigan witnessed in Beverly Hills.

Rattigan was astonished at his friend's 'great ability [. . .] to feign
indifference: when Kay was ill, even desperately sick, he would
still go off and play golf with me and be perfectly calm. I have
never seen such fortitude'.[7] One might quibble at some of
Harrison's choices, yet there is no doubting the intensity of his
feelings for his dying wife and within the marital conventions of
the 1950s his decision can be seen as generous both in its refusal
to share the burden of knowledge and in his commitment to easing
his wife's final years. Harrison himself described the period
between the diagnosis and Kendall's death in September 1959 as
'without doubt the worst and yet the best years of my life'.[8]

With the funeral over, Rattigan invited Harrison to stay with him
at his home in Sunningdale. When even golf failed to provide
adequate distraction from Harrison's grief, they went for a holiday
to Cannes together. Rattigan broached the idea of writing a play
about a husband concealing his wife's terminal illness from her.
But Harrison felt it was too early, and in December 1959, when a
story about the proposed play appeared in the *Evening Standard*,
Rattigan was forced to issue a denial, employing the politician's
caveat that he would not be writing such a play in the 'foreseeable
future'.[9] Instead, Rattigan promised to give Harrison an opportunity to throw himself into work, offering to write a new play, a
double bill comprising two plays, *Like Father* and *Like Son*, with
good leading roles for his friend.

This double bill turned into two separate plays. A draft of the first,
Like Father, was completed in October 1960. Although it has
never been performed, it has its interest as one of the many
tributaries that fed into the writing of *In Praise of Love*.

The play is set in the Bloomsbury residence of Bert Leavenworth,
an anti-establishment beatnik artist. Ferociously hostile to all
conventional values, he is shocked to discover the conventionality
of his son, Augustus, who does not drink or take drugs, wants to
become a chartered accountant, and plans to marry an upper-class
woman, Margaret Mackenzie, whose father fought for Franco in
the Spanish Civil War. A mildly farcical plot eventually finds the
two fathers joining forces.

The comedy derives from a rather relentless device of reversing
conventional attitudes; Bert is outraged to discover that his son goes
to church; Augustus makes himself look *less* presentable before
he'll meet his father, is later forced stammeringly to confess that
he has not slept with his girlfriend, and so on. The wit is strained,
and the plot predictable; in this raw first draft, the father seems
colourlessly decadent, and the son merely priggish.

It does, however, offer evidence of Rattigan's wounded reaction
to his dismissal by the New Wave. Bert has painted a gloomy

picture, entitled 'Aldermaston', which places him alongside the
Royal Court writers who famously joined the Aldermaston
marches that inaugurated the Campaign for Nuclear Disarmament.
Much of *Like Father* suggests that Rattigan had, in the character
of Bert, waspishly tried to imagine a middle-aged Jimmy Porter,
the anti-hero of Osborne's *Look Back in Anger*. Bert is even
described as 'a bit "the thirties" [. . .] sort of emotionally fixed
around that time',[10] the same era to which Porter casts envious
backward glances. Through his characters, Rattigan rebuts this
position at much the same level of lamentable simplicity that
pervaded *Joie de Vivre,* the disastrous musical version of *French
Without Tears* which had opened earlier that year, and which
included his complacent response to the Angry Decade, the song,
'I'm sorry – but I'm happy'.

The kind of finger-wagging that Rattigan usually cut out of later
drafts is in abundance in this piece, which dabbles a heavy hand
in the pool of cultural politics. Despite Rattigan's reputation, he
rarely wrote society farce, and when he did, he usually did so
badly. *Like Father* reads like inferior post-war Coward, an
unhappy amalgam of *Relative Values* and *Nude with Violin*.
Rattigan may have recognised this, because after a small rewrite,
the play was never even sent to a producer. What gives a
fascinating insight into Rattigan's craft as a playwright is that so
many of the threads of this earlier piece are woven into *In Praise
of Love*, and with so immeasurably greater an effect. The other
half of this double bill, *Like Son*, eventually became *Man and Boy*.
But Rex Harrison brusquely turned it down, and the eventual
production ran for only 69 performances.

Rattigan was having a bad 1960s. The failure of *Man and Boy* was
a particularly hard blow, since Rattigan thought it was potentially
the last chance to restore his reputation in the face of critical and
theatrical hostility. He took to drinking heavily, and would strike a
repetitively querulous tone in interviews, trying to justify his
approach to playwriting against the less graceful forms pursued by
Osborne, Wesker, and Arden. In Spring 1966, he announced his
intention to become a tax exile, moving to Bermuda, a decision
taken partly for financial reasons, but also out of impotent
petulance in the face of a culture that seemed to have rejected him.

Rattigan's sense that *Man and Boy* may have been his last chance
came not merely from feeling that he was swimming against the
theatrical tide but also from his belief that he had only a matter of
months to live. In April 1963, staying at one of his villas in Ischia,
Rattigan suffered recurrent headaches, weight loss, and a sore
throat he could not shake off. He sought medical advice, but the
answer was the one he most dreaded: he had leukemia, the same
condition from which Kay Kendall had died.

However, an intensive course of cortisone seemed to be working; his physical health revived, and the diagnosis appeared to have been a false alarm. Rattigan threw himself into his self-imposed exile, funding his accustomed lifestyle by taking lucrative contracts to write film scripts, the best of which were never made, while his place in theatrical memory receded further and further. The death of his mother in April 1971, and his *ennui* at churning out film scripts to order, prompted a return to England. Perhaps he also realised that his decision to leave had been inspired by pique, though it was also suggested, to Rattigan's fury, that his return home was prompted by the award of a knighthood in June 1971. A year later, however, Rattigan's health worsened again and a new set of tests demonstrated what Rattigan had feared. The leukemia had only been in remission: he was indeed dying.

A combination of the newly-confirmed diagnosis, and a feeling that his imminent demise freed him from his self-denying ordinance, led him to reconsider the idea he fleetingly proposed to Rex Harrison in Cannes a decade earlier. Rattigan's next and perhaps last play would take its inspiration from Harrison's compassionate deception of Kay Kendall.[11] But the play that resulted, *In Praise of Love*, is not an impersonal piece of observation; it is an agonized examination of the codes and decorum by which he had lived his whole life, in and out of the theatre.

Rattigan moved back into his bachelor apartment in the Albany, London, and began writing. The play, *After Lydia*, was conceived by Rattigan as a miniature, a one-act piece, and to make up a full programme he returned to the formula that had twice proved so successful: a double bill. *After Lydia* would cohabit the evening with another one-act play, *Before Dawn*[12] Rattigan's most consistent producer had been the legendary 'Binkie' Beaumont of H.M. Tennent Ltd, the man who had whimsically suggested that Rattigan write a comedy about death; despite Beaumont having turned down both previous double bills, fearing the proposition to be uncommercial, in early Spring 1973, Rattigan sent him the new plays. Beaumont phoned Rattigan to suggest Celia Johnson for Lydia, if the part was rewritten to make her an Englishwoman, and John Gielgud for Sebastian. Rattigan dismissed both suggestions, and the two determined to talk further. This would never happen, because the next morning, 23 March 1973, Rattigan received a telephone call informing him that Beaumont had died in the night.[13]

Beaumont's death, somehow turned by most obituary-writers into a rather heartening indication that an era of elegant emotional duplicity in British theatre had finally passed, was a blow to Rattigan, both personally and professionally. Nonetheless, preparations for the production rumbled on. Rattigan persuaded John Dexter to direct the plays. They met in June, and, after

Dexter insisted on some time to work with Rattigan on the texts, they took themselves off to Cannes – the place where the idea for the play was first mooted. As a contemporary news report describes it:

> Dexter was an early riser and Rattigan a late-night writer. They worked mainly before or after dinner and Rattigan would then work away into the night and when Dexter came down in the morning he'd find the rewrites waiting with his orange juice. Both seemed happy with the collaboration. 'I hope we'll continue working together in the future,' said Rattigan.[14]

They never did, and it was surprising that they ever worked together at all, coming as they did from very different theatrical backgrounds. Dexter had been an early star of the Royal Court, making his name directing the Wesker trilogy. He was, in fact, ambivalent about taking on the assignment. In August 1973 he wrote to Stephen Sondheim: 'You may have heard, I am doing a double bill by Terence Rattigan almost immediately. I can see the disapproving look on your face but I think they are very good,' rather spoiling this stoutness of this defence by adding that it would make him a good deal of money.[15] Despite this, their collaboration yielded a spare, tautly-constructed and compelling piece of work.

A note, however, on *Before Dawn*. It is extraordinary that Rattigan should have decided to accompany one of the best things he ever wrote with one of the very worst, but the judgement seems undeniable. *Before Dawn* is a farcical reworking of Victorien Sardou's *La Tosca* (1887), better known for Puccini's operatic adaptation, *Tosca,* in 1900. What was heightened, passionate, tragic in the opera becomes slender, half-hearted and bathetic in Rattigan's hands. In the original, the evil Scarpia tells the beautiful Tosca that if she will consent to sleep with him, he will spare the life of her lover, Cavaradossi, by staging a faked execution. As Tosca appears to succumb to Scarpia's embrace, she stabs him with a secreted knife. This does not save Cavaradossi, though, and the execution is anything but faked. In despair and spotted by the guard, Tosca hurls herself from the castle battlements. In Rattigan's version, as Tosca plunges the knife, she discovers that Scarpia is wearing a protective vest. Tosca's modesty is preserved, however, by the discovery of Scarpia's impotence. He is in fact only spiritually attracted her, being rather more interested in the young male artist, Angelotti, and he arranges a successful faked execution for the two lovers, who can therefore make good their escape. Unlike his previous double bill, *Separate Tables,* the two plays were by no means equal, and Rattigan clearly thought the piece little more than a trifle, subtitling *Before Dawn* in the programme 'A Divertimento (with apologies to the neglected ghost of Victorien Sardou)', and one might generously interpret this as an affectionate nod to one of the great designers of the well-made play. It is hard to disagree, however, with Charles Lewsen's remark in *The Times* that 'if I were the neglected ghost of Victorien Sardou, I should quietly ignore the impertinence'.

It is ironic that Rattigan's tribute should have been so half-hearted, because its companion piece, *In Praise of Love* (as *After Lydia* eventually became[16]), is Rattigan's last attempt at a well-made play and one of his best, in which he invests those mechanics with a wealth of intense personal feeling.

The moral dilemma that rampages through the stately passageways of *In Praise of Love* is between virtuous honesty and altruistic concealment. The debate had been put on stage a century earlier by a playwright deeply influential on the young Rattigan; in Henrik Ibsen's *The Wild Duck* (1885), Gregers Werle, the champion of *den ideale fordring* (the claim of the ideal, or absolute standards of honesty), is pitted against the dissolute Dr Relling, with his faith in *livsløgnen* (the life-lie, the avoidance of pain through compassionate untruths). Traces of *The Wild Duck*'s climactic and unresolved debate echo through this play, especially in the dispute between Joey and Lydia. Joey's unblinking commitment to telling the truth – 'honesty, in this life, is just about the only thing that matters' (p. 69) – is pitted against Lydia and Sebastian's belief in the life-lie.

But this is not a play of serene impersonal debate. The question was of intense personal concern to Rattigan. By 1973, he had already spent over fifteen years in a new theatrical climate which scorned his work for artificiality, formal conservatism, and emotional repression. In 1970, the countercultural theatre maker and critic, Albert Hunt, had savaged Rattigan's work for its 'facile knowingness', a smug sense that 'every complexity can be explained away, every facet of human experience reduced to a simple matter of manipulation [. . .] a world in which everything can be solved by a little craftsmanship'.[17] Rattigan had not been forgiven for his uncompromising defence of plot construction, of the craft of dramatic storytelling; at a time when traditional dramaturgy, genres and forms were being discarded and reworked in Arts Labs and alternative theatre venues around the country, he was an easy target.

In Praise of Love specifically conjoins the debate in the subplot of Joey's play. We discover very little about it, but what we do hear positions it in Hunt's camp rather than Rattigan's. The play is a political piece, cast in a faintly absurdist form; or, as Sebastian off-handedly describes it, a 'piece of pseudo-Kafka crap' (p. 20). (In earlier drafts, the play was clearly ultra-leftist in its politics, though this made nonsense of the political debates between liberal

son and communist father.[18]) We also discover that it was submitted for a series 'limited to plays by authors under twenty-one'
(p. 20). One of the things that characterised the new theatrical
priorities of the fifties and sixties was what John Osborne called a
'cachet in youth'.[19] Joey betrays the emotional preferences of the
post-1956 generation when he quibbles at his mother crying at the
play: 'it's really supposed to make one angry' (p. 80). Rattigan
had often criticised both plays of ideas and the theatre of the absurd,
and the combination is designed to exemplify the opposite dramaturgical pole to *In Praise of Love*. As we shall see, however, this is
a precarious distinction, which the play works hard to break down.

The accusation of dishonesty had another dimension. For Rattigan
the first sign of shifting theatrical tides came in 1958 with reviews
of his play, *Variation on a Theme*, one of which was headlined,
'Are Things What They Seem?'[20] The secret subject of the play
which the critics believed they had detected was homosexuality. It
was an accusation which would dog Rattigan's plays long after his
death. In 1982, reviewing a revival of *In Praise of Love*, Nicholas
de Jongh noted the play's criticism of the 'failure to face up to
one's own emotions', but added curtly that 'sadly he spent half a
lifetime in submission to the very kind of reticence he deplored'.[21]
It is quite unreasonable to have expected Rattigan to identify his
sexuality to a still largely hostile public, in a society where
homosexual acts were illegal, yet charges of theatrical dishonesty
were rife amongst leading figures of the new wave.[22]

The play is informed by Rattigan's pitiless examination of the
values and codes by which he lived his life. In 1974 Hamish
Hamilton paid Rattigan a £5000 advance for an autobiography,
provisionally titled *Without Tears*.[23] He never wrote it but *In
Praise of Love* is saturated with hints and fragments of Rattigan's
own life, and echoes of his earlier plays. This might lead one to
imagine that *In Praise of Love* is a piece of special pleading,
narrowly tied to the plight of its author. It is true, as Michael
Darlow puts it, that the play 'reads like a testament, a final
drawing together of the personal strands of Rattigan's drama'.[24]
But it is the very intensity of the personal feeling in the play
which gives a broader emotional life to the unusually careful and
meticulous plotting.

The play is unusual in Rattigan's oeuvre in having relatively little
reference to homosexuality. Sebastian and Mark have a slightly
campy relationship, and there are a couple of references to
confusions between kings and queens, or Suzie and Sammy
Wongs. But otherwise it is a play without the sexual explicitness
of *Man and Boy*, the allegorical coding of *Separate Tables*, or the
fierce sexual passions of *The Deep Blue Sea*. Indeed, one senses
that showing Sebastian and Lydia's relationship at a time when

sex has ceased to play a role is deliberate: the love that is traced out between them has a platonic quality. As Rattigan suggested shortly before the premiere, the play concerns 'spiritual love'.[25]

But the theme is gently suggested in the motif of pretending and disguise that reverberates through the play. In different ways, all of the characters pretend to be someone they are not. Sebastian is, of course, pretending not to care for his wife. But his left-wing politics also seem rather fraudulent, since he strike-breaks, buys tickets for a cricket match against South Africa, accepts an OBE, and seems to know nothing about the communist candidate he is supposedly supporting in the upcoming by-election. Lydia perpetrates an impressive string of minor deceptions: she imper-sonates her doctor's receptionist to discover her test results; she plays at being a simple Estonian woman with poor English at the chemist and with the student doctors. More significantly, during the war she escaped being murdered by a Nazi firing squad by pretending to be dead, a performance which inversely parallels her current pretence that she is not dying. Mark also pretends to be Sebastian as part of the cover story Lydia has arranged when Sebastian fails to appear for Joey's broadcast. At one point Lydia addresses him as 'Marcus Waldt', rather than the anglicized 'Mark Walters', a discreet alteration reflecting the other benign decep-tions in the play. Even the idealistic truth-teller Joey has decided to bill himself in his play's credits as 'Joseph', because 'it sounds more like a writer' (p. 79).

This web of large and small deceptions all reinforce the central concealments of the play: Sebastian's and Lydia's withholding of information about her illness, and their no less significant refusal to profess their love for each other. But the list offered is also im-portant because immediately it is clear that there are distinctions to be drawn between kinds of deceit. While we may sympathise, it is difficult entirely to approve of Sebastian's affair with Prunella Larkin, and it is hardly of a piece with Lydia's literal life-lie, playing dead in a Nazi mass grave.

There was a class basis to the attacks on Rattigan. It was the artificial world of upper-middle-class manners which seemed so anachronistic to the new generation. Rattigan deals directly with this issue, and it forms an important strand to the notion of concealment. We are told that Sebastian believes in William of Wykeham's tenet 'Manners Makyth Man', the motto of his alma mater, Winchester School. This is curious, given Sebastian's rather unmannerly behaviour with his wife, though perhaps this should be seen as a studied insouciance, a middle-class inclination to abstain from overt emotional display. Early in the play, Lydia confides in Mark the social embarrassment she once caused by emotionally retelling her wartime experiences. 'Oh damn the

English!' she cries. 'Sometimes I think that their bad form doesn't just lie in revealing their emotions, it's in having any at all' (p. 31). It was often this register in which the generation of playwrights before Rattigan wrote, and it was Lydia's accusation that underlay his rejection by the generation that came after him.

Rattigan was historically caught between those two eras of emotional *sang froid* and angry outpouring. While a writer like Coward generates much of his sympathetic humour from the ability to be unflappable in a crisis, Rattigan's use of this tone is tainted with melancholy. Towards the end of the play, we discover that Sebastian's carelessness is in fact the mark of a tremendous effort to prevent his true feelings coming out, rather than a sign of their absence. We can now understand his obsession with linguistic form – he corrects everyone's grammar, idioms, pronunciation, and is fervent in his organisation of the library shelves – as an image of his attempt to keep his house in order. The house comes to represent his own mind; before any character has appeared before us, we hear a coded signal of Sebastian's self-censorship: as the curtain rises, his typewriter is heard clattering in his study 'with long pauses between short bouts, usually followed by unmistakeable sounds of angry erasure' (p. 5). In retrospect we can see a glimpse of the pain underlying his cool demeanour in his comic admission that he spends hours 'screaming [. . .] for someone to care' in the smallest room in the house (p. 18).

While the bulk of the play is proceeding we get very little sense of his feelings, except in the curious moment that ends Act One. Lydia has been drinking and is about to begin preparing dinner when she suffers a minor stroke, halting suddenly and clutching at the banister. 'Sebastian moves with extraordinary quickness to reach her before Joey, whom he roughly pushes back so that he nearly falls' (p. 59). The moment jars with our understanding of Sebastian at this point, the urgency of his action belying his posture of indifference. Immediately though, Sebastian transforms his action into one of sardonic deprecation, as he implies that she is drunk and helps her up the stairs. This subtle transformation forestalls our complete realisation of his feelings, but later we see it repeated when Sebastian is interrupted by Lydia in his conversation with Mark. He has told Mark about his true knowledge and his real feelings, and he breaks down in tears contemplating life after Lydia. But as his wife enters, he 'jumps up from his chair and turns his back, adroitly transforming emotion into huffiness' (p. 94). This revelation that his inattentiveness is all a performance opens up the space between emotional expression and concealment, and deepens our understanding of that maligned social register.

There are defences of polite dissembling. Lydia has learned the value of polite concealment. Her impetuous claim that the British see having emotions as bad form is subtly adjusted through the play. She defends white lies to Joey, remarking that Mark's apparent enthusiasm for watching his play might not strictly reflect his real feelings, and then tricks Joey into issuing the same kind of polite lie that he had been so opposed to (p. 77). But the play does not defend all kinds of concealment: as Sebastian admits to Mark, 'Do you know what "le vice Anglais" – the English vice – really is? Not flagellation, not pederasty – whatever the French believe it to be. It's our refusal to admit to our emotions. We think they demean us, I suppose' (p. 94). Yet, at the end of the play, it is emotional honesty that would be sentimental, and he carefully denies us the revelation scene.

After his first entrance, Sebastian's first move is towards the bookcase, where he soon begins to find a number of volumes out of place. At one point he finds 'Norman Mailer in the poetry section. Why?' (p. 7). The joke of finding that most prosaic of novelists amongst the verse is a good one, though Rattigan too has been faulted for the flat inelegance of some of his dialogue.[26] But we should not be looking to the dialogue for the most poetically-wrought elements of the play. As in the final scene of *Separate Tables*, an extraordinarily emotional and dramatic scene played entirely in small talk,[27] it is in the construction of the plot that Rattigan creates the most graceful vehicle for exploring the ethics of truth-telling.

There are three major revelations in the play which distribute knowledge between characters and the audience, and with each Rattigan directs and misdirects our attention. Not long into the play, Lydia's revelation of her diagnosis pulls our sympathies away from Sebastian, whom we criticize much as Rattigan himself had been criticized, for emotional sterility. His amusing foibles now seem more like thoughtless disregard. However, towards the end of the play, Sebastian also tells Mark that he knows about Lydia's illness. Absurdly, now, both Sebastian and Lydia know the truth but have tried to conceal it from the other because neither wishes to let on how in love they really are. It is a twist which echoes the opening of the play, with Lydia's unexplained but evident physical distress and Sebastian's equally unexplained vague unconcern, two people locked together in mysterious mutual isolation. Rattigan's dialogue may seem flat on the printed page, but in performance the iron structure of the play charges and animates some of the simplest utterances. In a play which uses several lines from Shakespeare, one of the most heart-rendingly beautiful moments is Sebastian's simple, artless admission: 'But, oh Mark, life without Lydia will be such unending misery' (p. 94). Rattigan always knew the theatrical virtue of the plain sentence.

The third revelation takes this even further. Mark breaks the impasse by suggesting that Lydia might extend the library steps to look in a hatbox on a high shelf. There she finds the real medical reports which Sebastian has been hiding. Of course, hidden documents have always been a staple of the well-made play – Susan Rusinko, in a reference to another early master of the form, calls this a 'small piece of Scribean carpentry'[28] – but Rattigan has given it an original twist. The discovery of letters or diaries which incriminate their authors gives the playwright a dramaturgical problem: break the plausibility of the scene by having them read aloud, or split the exposition of their contents from the character's reaction by taking them offstage to be read. But here it is not the contents which we or Lydia are interested in, it is the fact of their existence. The artful structure of the play reaches its climax in this single moment, as Lydia discovers that Sebastian loves her.

The moment is emblematic of the strength and complexity of Rattigan's dramaturgy, artfully and subtly underlining the play's debate. Again it is a silent scene, but one in which we glimpse a wealth of emotion perceived and felt. The hat box itself is an interesting choice; it contained the top hat that Sebastian wore to receive his OBE, and thus represents not just the cerebral life of the writer-critic, but also the old-fashioned establishment stuffiness for which Rattigan was often condemned. But in the hat box, Lydia gets an insight into Sebastian's heart. Beneath the formality lies a compassion, between the indifferent lines of the medical reports a reaching-out of feeling. We look at Sebastian now through Lydia's eyes. At the very end of the play, Lydia lingers on the stairs watching her husband, and we are told that she 'smiles. In fact, radiantly' (p. 104). It's another silent moment, unnoticed by anyone on stage, and yet as Rattigan told Julie Harris who played Lydia on Broadway, 'it's the most important line in the play'.[29]

Historically caught between two theatrical registers, Rattigan shows us the devastating human consequences of living in this gap between emotion concealed and emotion expressed. It is not their affectation of emotional nonchalance that makes Rattigan's plays distinctive but rather – as in Joan's suicide in *After the Dance*, Andrew's breakdown in *The Browning Version*, and Hester's pleas to her lover in *The Deep Blue Sea* – the great wells of emotion that erupt through the years of sedimented social restraint. By letting us into these concealed passions, the subterranean realm in which Rattigan's plays have always had their profoundest effects, he shows us the tragedy and the complexity of this English malaise.

This is a personal play, then; not a defence but an explanation of his own life. And while Rattigan's own concerns can be detected here, he has not created a single mouthpiece for his own views. Some of the lightness and subtlety of the play may derive from the way that Rattigan has invested *all* the characters with elements of himself. Sebastian is a writer whose best work is widely thought to have been written in the forties; recently honoured, he uneasily recognises that his radicalism may have been compromised by his drift towards the establishment, and he lives a life of emotional concealment. But Lydia also connects with Rattigan's own experience; in the first versions of the play, her illness was leukemia, the same illness from which Rattigan was suffering, and which he had also tried to conceal. Joey is in many ways a portrait of the young Rattigan; a political activist, aspiring playwright, close to his mother, distant from his father. Mark lives in Eaton Square, where Rattigan once had a flat, and has been met with great commercial success, though critical neglect.

The alliances and disagreements between these figures suggest ambiguities and conflicts in Rattigan's own life. Even the opposition between Mark's blockbusters and Joey's clumsily heartfelt agitprop is spanned in Rattigan's own life. In the first performed draft, Sebastian compares two lines about death from Shakespeare, adding: 'the first one is Royal Court, but that one is pure Shaftesbury Avenue. Cosy, commercial and comforting'.[30] In this play, Rattigan perhaps tries to link the rawness and seriousness of the Royal Court, home of the New Wave, with the artful formality of the commercial tradition. The great book that Sebastian threatens to write is possibly to be his account of his last months with Lydia; after all, Rattigan, on learning that his leukemia was advancing, 'repeatedly told Binkie Beaumont and other close friends, all that really mattered to him was to write one great play before he died'.[31]

There are two substantially different versions of *In Praise of Love*.[32] The first version, performed as *After Lydia* alongside *Before Dawn*, is a brisk piece, designed to be played in one headlong rush, as it was at the Duchess Theatre in 1973. For the two leads Joan Greenwood and Donald Sinden were chosen. Greenwood was a distinguished and versatile film and theatre actor, noted for her huskily musical voice and wide-eyed pathos in both comic and tragic roles. Sinden was an accomplished classical actor, whose unfortunate introduction to Rattigan had been playing in the disastrous *Joie de Vivre*. Sebastian Cruttwell was to be a much more rewarding part for him. The designer, Desmond Heeley, built a cluttered layered set, hemmed in by tall bookcases whose impassive spines glared inwardly onto the action, emphasising Sebastian's claustrophobic emotional charade.

Greenwood and Sinden were praised by the critics. J.C. Trewin admired Greenwood's voice, 'like the tinkling of old lustres', and thought that Donald Sinden's performance 'rises to those moments when the man's grief overwhelms him utterly and he crumples: that is playing to remember, and remember it we shall'. John Barber in the *Daily Telegraph* detected the subtlety of its structure, declaring that it 'glides craftily forward, avoiding by the narrowest of margins both the nets of artifice and the shallows of sentimentality'. Others were more hostile, though Jane Gaskell in the *Daily Mail* was surely alone in preferring the curtain raiser. Most critics seem to have been fatally disheartened by the flimsiness of *Before Dawn* and gave at best only grudging approval to *After Lydia*. Milton Shulman in the *Evening Standard* spoke for many at the time in believing that the play was 'not likely to be counted amongst his most important works'.

Though deeply disappointed, Rattigan was less nervous of the critics than the response of an old friend. Rex Harrison came to see *In Praise of Love* with his fifth wife, Elizabeth. He appeared to have been pleased by the portrayal, and when plans for a Broadway production emerged, he indicated a provisional willingness to take on the part. In his autobiography, however, Harrison recalls some apprehension: 'I was full of trepidation about doing a story which sailed so close to the wind of my own life and my own private pain'.[33] So he was alarmed to see the *Daily Mail* jump the gun, announcing his agreement and luridly reminding its readers of the proximity of the action of the play to events in Harrison's life with Kay Kendall. Rattigan responded with a ten-page letter, trying to pacify him and reassure him about the play. The contents of this letter are worth examining in some detail, because they reveal the seed of a disagreement which would spill out into furious rows after the show opened in New York.

Rattigan apologises for the premature announcement in the press, and tries to dismiss the piece as 'gossip-writer's muck' that no one would remember.[34] The unfortunate incident gives Rattigan an opportunity to make some things clear: 'top of the list – *point number one*, namely: Sebastian Cruttwell is NOT Rex Harrison: Rex Harrison, to be Sebastian Cruttwell on stage, must play a character part, i.e. he must do everything to avoid any identification by the audience of the two totally dissimilar characters'. He acknowledges that an audience is likely to know something of Harrison's marriage with Kendall (by the time the play opened, Harrison had published the first version of his autobiography, in which he discussed the relationship in great detail). But he adds, 'I'm not saying that it's going to [be] easy for you – or for me, when I re-write – to stop an audience making that sentimental, wrong-headed and, I believe, utterly disastrous identification; but somehow we still have to do it...'.

To reinforce the point, he lists the differences between Sebastian's and Rex's situations, emphasising the fact that Lydia knows about her illness, while Kay died in blissful ignorance. In this, Rattigan was being politely disingenuous. He had always held the private view that Kendall had worked out exactly what was going on. As Harrison's biographer puts it, 'He always believed that Kay was giving Rex strength by refusing to acknowledge that her illness was terminal. She and Rex, in his opinion, knew how to play that kind of scene together. They were both of them keeping reality at bay. Just as they made the unreality of stage and screen a way of earning a living, it was also the way they faced the prospect of Kay's dying'.[35]

It was important for Rattigan to stress the differences between his character and its real-life source, because Harrison had evidently objected to what he felt was a portrait of himself as an 'uncaring shit'. Harrison wanted it signalled from the start that he was acting from the highest motives. Rattigan is polite but firm in his refusal: 'that "caringness" must – repeat MUST – come as a surprise – or, at least, creep up very belatedly – because if he is shown *early on* as "caring", then we have no play'. He was right, of course, since the play's structural dynamics depend on the change of sympathies at the end. Rattigan ended the letter with a flattering restatement: 'Sebastian is *not* Rex Harrison. (I would never so have insulted my friend.) Rex Harrison will be a *magical* Sebastian – but that means a Sebastian produced by Rex Harrison's own particular brand of theatrical magic . . . which is unsurpassable, unsurpassed, but not Rex Harrison just being Rex. (I'll go into sonnet form if I don't shut up.) Much, much love, Terry'.

Rattigan then spent a week at Harrison's favourite Italian resort, Portofino, preparing rewrites to lengthen the piece. This involved amplifying Lydia's war record and letting us see Lydia persuade Joey to stay with his father while she is away. Rattigan also removes some of the more specifically British references, and changed the illness from leukemia to polyarteritis nodosa, probably to put further distance between Lydia and Kay.[36] Wisely he omitted reference to the Hippocratic oath, which raises troubling questions of the doctor's plausibility. For the female lead, various names were suggested, including, most improbably, Bette Davis.[37] Finally, Julie Harris, after turning the part down once, agreed to play Lydia. Rattigan had developed pneumonia while canvassing (like Joey) for the Liberal Party, and his doctor had forbidden him to travel. As a result he was unable to attend the rehearsals.

Now, Rex Harrison, in 1974, was one of the biggest stars in the world. His performance in *My Fair Lady* had made him a household name. He believed, and was perhaps right to believe, that audiences came to see him, not the character, and was always careful to maintain his star persona on stage. In 1950, he had turned down the lead in Rattigan's *Who is Sylvia?* not wanting to play a philanderer, despite offstage antics which had earned him the nickname 'Sexy Rexy'. Some years later when he turned down the part of the homosexual banker in *Man and Boy*, he crudely declared himself disinclined to be seen as part of a 'brotherhood of buggers'.[38] These instances should have alerted Rattigan to the fact that Harrison had no intention of listening to the cautions in his letter. The gravitational pull of his own experiences led him simply to overwrite the part with the carefully cultivated public image of his own life with Kendall. When Rattigan finally was able to travel to New York, only two days before opening night, he discovered a caring, kindly Sebastian, who from the very start inspected his wife's medical reports with enormous care, and thus made a nonsense of the play.

Rattigan was furious but powerless in the face of Harrison's star status. Unable to prevent him from adding absurd new pieces of charming business (some of it involving leaving the stage and falling over a bicycle), or trying to upstage and cut the lines of Julie Harris, Rattigan returned to London. The play opened at the Morosco Theatre on Broadway on 10 December 1974, to generally favourable reviews; Rex Reed in the *Daily News* called it 'the kind of play Broadway has been waiting for – an extraordinary evening of rare perfection'.[39] Not even the rare perfection of such a review can have comforted Rattigan knowing how savagely Harrison's unbalancing of his structure had misrepresented the play. Particularly galling must have been the *New Yorker*'s praise: 'a flicker of an eyelid, an infinitesimal clearing of the throat, and – presto! – a pinch of wit becomes an epigram. The skimpier the play, the more resourceful Mr Harrison'.[40]

In March 1976, the play was beautifully revived for Anglia Television, directed by Alvin Rakoff, with Claire Bloom and Kenneth More; there was also an excellent BBC radio production with Anthony Quayle and Muriel Pavlow, directed by Peter King. A touring production in October 1977, with Richard Todd and Virginia Stride, failed to come into London. And that seemed to be that. A month later, on 30 November, believing his most agonized theatrical self-examination had been tidily forgotten, Rattigan finally succumbed to the leukemia he had been fighting for a decade.

Five years later, on 1 March 1982, *In Praise of Love* was revived by Stewart Trotter at the King's Head, the stage on which the same director's dramatic rediscovery of *The Browning Version* in 1976 had marked a brief revival in its author's reputation. This was a new version of *In Praise of Love,* since Rattigan, unable to

leave the play alone, had made further revisions of the expanded
New York text for publication. Many critics were surprised by the
play's 'quite heart-stopping moments of truth and grief', in
Nicholas de Jongh's phrase. William Franklyn perhaps overplayed
Sebastian's irascibility, not entirely rising to the moment of
epiphany with Mark, though Isabel Dean's Lydia, portrayed with
burdened restraint perforated by moments of radiant joy, was
widely praised. After the 1973 premiere, which had seen the play
scorned for domestic sentimentality, it is striking to read Irving
Wardle's description of its fine 'workmanship; played with wit
and the fire of old wounds'.

Rattigan's old friend, Freddie Young, loyally ended his review in
the *Financial Times* with the words, 'if this is a symptom of the
rumoured Rattigan revival, it is a very welcome one'. In fact, no
such revival transpired, and productions of Rattigan's work
remained thin on the ground until the early 1990s. A BBC
television production of *After the Dance* in 1992 and, in particular,
the Almeida's haunting revival of *The Deep Blue Sea* at the
beginning of 1993 led a string of producers to re-examine
Rattigan's work. Peter Hall directed *Separate Tables* at the Albery
Theatre in 1993, and 1994 saw West End and film versions of *The
Browning Version,* and *The Winslow Boy* on Shaftesbury Avenue.
In Praise of Love followed on 6 March 1995, directed by Richard
Olivier at the Apollo Theatre, and starring Peter Bowles and Lisa
Harrow as Sebastian and Lydia. A further revival, with Julian
Glover and Isla Blair, directed by Deborah Bruce, toured the UK
during January to March 2001.

Critics were better disposed to accept Rattigan after two years of
well-handled revivals. In *Today*, Bill Hagerty praised Olivier's
production as a 'masterful interpretation of a master-craftsman's
last major play'. (Neil Bartlett's magnificent rediscovery of *Cause
Célèbre* was still to come.) Only Coveney in the *Observer* was
unrepentant. For most, the appearance of cloying sentimentality
had yielded to an stinging emotional realism; 'it ought to help to
extinguish the idea, if it is still lurking about,' wrote John Peter
in the *Sunday Times*, 'that [Rattigan] was a superficial boulevard
dramatist who bought his seriousness or his emotions cheap'.
His aching compassion was compared favourably with the more
waspish wit of Coward's *Design for Living,* then running at the
Globe in a revamped, allegedly gay-friendly production: 'where
Coward is spiteful, Rattigan is compassionate,' wrote Hagerty.
'Where Coward relishes superiority, Rattigan sympathises with the
lonely and the inadequate'. Bowles was widely praised for having
balanced the coldness with an underlying anguish, and Jack Tinker
praised Lisa Harrow's 'haunting performance'. It was heartening
to see the play understood as taking emotional reticence as its
subject, not its theatrical register, in Paul Taylor's declaration that

'it demonstrates that Rattigan is not so much the victim of English repression as one of its most skilled anatomists'.[41]

Even so, perhaps *In Praise of Love* has yet to receive a production which confronts the emotional wilderness lying beyond the box-set trappings of its first production. The neatness of the play can be distracting to a contemporary audience, attuned to a greater looseness of form and a more challenging rawness of emotion. These elements remain to be tapped by a staging which can directly draw from the enormous reserves of bitter self-recrimination and concealed romantic yearning that tears through the formality of this play. *In Praise of Love* is, in many ways, Rattigan's testament, but a testament to the cruel paradoxes of his emotional life, an unsentimental anatomisation of sentiment, a play in praise of the late dawning of love.

Notes

1. All reviews of the 1973 production, here and subsequently, quoted from the Production File for *In Praise of Love*. Duchess Theatre. 27 September 1973, in the Theatre Museum, London.

2. Penelope Gilliatt famously declared in 1959 that 'one of the most characteristic sounds of the English Sunday is Harold Hobson barking up the wrong tree', in: 'A Consideration of Critics' *Encore: The Voice of Vital Theatre.* vi, 5 (November-December 1959), pp. 27.

3. I have run together passages from two reviews by Hobson, dated 30 September and 21 October 1973.

4. Geoffrey Wansell. *Terence Rattigan: A Biography*. London: Fourth Estate, 1995, p. 369.

5. David Lewin, 'The greatest, most loving role Rex Harrison has ever had to play...' *Daily Mail.* (22 October 1974), p. 7.

6. Rex Harrison. *Rex: An Autobiography.* London: Macmillan, 1974, p. 151.

7. Quoted in David Lewin, *op. cit.*

8. Rex Harrison, *op. cit.,* p. 152.

9. Alexander Walker. *Fatal Charm: The Life of Rex Harrison.* London: Weidenfeld & Nicolson, 1992, p. 232.

10. *Like Father* [Typescript, October 1960], Rattigan Papers: British Library, London, vol. cxxix, Add. Mss. 74416, I-24.

11. The wife of his friend, the producer Stephen Mitchell, had also died from leukaemia, without being told the truth of her diagnosis.

12. Even more confusingly, the titles were at one point announced to the press as *The Exile* and *Vittoria*. See *Daily Telegraph*, 4 September 1973.

13. Richard Huggett. *Binkie Beaumont: Eminence Grise of the West End Theatre 1933-1973*. London: Hodder & Stoughton, 1989, p. 23.

14. 'Why The English Lose At Love' *Evening Standard*, 7 September 1973.

15. John Dexter. *The Honourable Beast: A Posthumous Autobiography.* London: Nick Hern Books, 1993, pp. 45-46. Two months later, after the reviews appeared, he retreated from his earlier praise, now seeming to feel that accepting the job had been akin to prostitution (p. 46).

16. Just as the double-bill of *The Browning Version* and *Harlequinade* were initially presented under the collective title *Playbill*, the new pairing of *Before Dawn* and *After Lydia* were offered as *In Praise of Love*. But while

Harlequinade is an amusing throwaway, *Before Dawn* actually seemed to detract from *After Lydia*. During the week of previews the producers alternated the order of plays, but settled on *Before Dawn* followed by *After Lydia* for the press night. But if *Before Dawn* had seemed flippantly bathetic after the agonies of *After Lydia*, placing the farce beforehand meant that the audience which returned from the interval were not well-disposed to the serious second half. Within a couple of weeks, Rattigan and his producers had attempted to limit the damage caused by the unappealing farce by retitling the second play *In Praise of Love*, to advertise its centrality to the evening. *Before Dawn* which had begun previews with the subtitle 'A Divertimento Without Music', and had limped into the press night as 'A Divertimento (with apologies to the neglected ghost of Victorien Sardou)' was finally downgraded even further as 'A Curtain Raiser'. When the play was produced in America, *In Praise of Love* was expanded and *Before Dawn* abandoned. It has never been performed professionally since, and *In Praise of Love*, unless explicitly stated, refers here to the Sebastian/Lydia play only, not the imprudent reworking of Sardou.

17. Albert Hunt. 'Danger: Craftsman at Work.' *New Society*. xvi, 424. (12 November 1970). p. 873.

18. *After Lydia* [Typescript, 1972], Rattigan Papers: British Library, vol. ccxi, Add. Ms. 74498, p. II-21.

19. John Osborne. *A Better Class of Person: An Autobiography, Vol 1: 1929-1956*. London: Faber and Faber, 1981, p. 22.

20. See General Introduction, p. xiii.

21. Reviews from King's Head production quoted from *Theatre Record*, ii, 5 (25 February-10 March 1982), pp. 107-110.

22. Osborne recalls George Devine, the first artistic director of the English Stage Company at the Royal Court, denouncing the 'blight of buggery' and the 'patent inadequacies of homosexual plays masquerading as plays about straight men and women.' John Osborne. *Almost a Gentleman: An Autobiography, Vol 2: 1955-1966*. London: Faber and Faber, 1991, pp. 9-10. See also Dan Rebellato. *1956 and All That: The Making of Modern British Drama*. London: Routledge, 1999, pp. 213-223.

23. Letter, 20 June 1974, Rattigan Papers: British Library, vol. ccliii, Add. Ms. 74540.

24. Michael Darlow. *Terence Rattigan: The Man and His Work*. London: Quartet, 2000, p. 431.

25. Quoted in 'Why The English Lose at Love' *op. cit.*

26. Note, however, that he steals the joke 'it'll be Greek to me – except that I can read Greek' (p. 11) from the most floridly 'poetic' of twentieth-century playwrights, Christopher Fry.

27. Terence Rattigan. *Separate Tables*. London: Nick Hern, 1999, pp. 107-113.

28. Susan Rusinko. *Terence Rattigan*. English Authors, 366. Boston: Twayne, 1983, p. 130. Eugène Scribe was a prolific nineteenth-century French playwright, usually identified as the inventor of the well-made play.

29. Darlow, *op. cit.,* p. 437.

30. *After Lydia* [Typescript, 1972], Rattigan Papers: British Library, vol. ccxi, Add. Ms. 74498, p. I-40.

31. Darlow, *op. cit.,* p. 420.

32. The Rattigan papers are in a considerably more disordered state for this than any other play, possibly owing to his failing health. There is an incomplete manuscript and a complete typescript of the first draft, and two sets of typescripts incorporating some minor amendments and variations. The play

seems to have emerged pretty much fully formed from the beginning, and as is usual with Rattigan, the key dramatic moments are identical through all successive drafts. There is then a series of changes and typescripts for the American production. The final version – the one published here – is a final revision published in the fourth volume of his *Collected Plays*. This was a posthumous volume, and contained small errors which we have corrected here. This edition contains the first definitive text for *In Praise of Love*.

33. Rex Harrison. *A Damned Serious Business*. London: Bantam, 1990, p. 210.

34. Terence Rattigan. Letter to Rex Harrison. 3 August 1974, Rattigan Papers: British Library, vol. ccxiv, Add. Ms. 74501.

35. Alexander Walker, *op. cit.,* p. 232.

36. In a letter to Harrison, Rattigan says 'the disease has in fact been very carefully researched by me and I think in many ways it works better than leukemia apart, of course, from its name'. Rattigan's research was all too evident in his rewrites, which initially featured a moment where Mark took a medical dictionary from his pocket and leadenly read out an entry. This graceless suggestion was thankfully abandoned. Terence Rattigan. Letter and rewrites to Rex Harrison. 12 July 1974, Rattigan Papers: British Library, vol. ccxiv, Add. Ms. 74501.

37. Michael Imison. Letter to Terence Rattigan. 29 January 1974, Rattigan Papers: British Library, vol ccxvii, Add. Ms. 74504. Imison tactfully submits that the ages of Sebastian and Joey would have to be somewhat adjusted.

38. Quoted in Darlow, *op. cit.,* p. 387.

39. Quoted in B. A. Young. *The Rattigan Version: Sir Terence Rattigan and the Theatre of Character*. London: Hamish Hamilton, 1986, p. 191.

40. Quoted in Walker, *op. cit.,* p. 349.

41. All reviews quoted from *Theatre Record*, xv, 5 (27 March 1995), pp. 275-280.

List of Rattigan's Produced Plays

Title	British Première	New York Première
First Episode (with Philip Heimann)	"Q" Theatre, Surrey, 11 Sept 1933, trans. Comedy Th, 26 January 1934	Ritz Theatre 17 September 1934
French Without Tears	Criterion Th, 6 Nov 1936	Henry Miller Th, 28 Sept 1937
After the Dance	St James's Th, 21 June 1939	
Follow My Leader (with Anthony Maurice, alias Tony Goldschmidt)	Apollo Th, 16 Jan 1940	
Grey Farm (with Hector Bolitho)		Hudson Th, 3 May 1940
Flare Path	Apollo Th, 13 Aug 1942	Henry Miller Th, 23 Dec 1942
While the Sun Shines	Globe Th, 24 Dec 1943	Lyceum Th, 19 Sept 1944
Love in Idleness	Lyric Th, 20 Dec 1944	Empire Th (as *O Mistress Mine*), 23 Jan 1946
The Winslow Boy	Lyric Th, 23 May 1946	Empire Th, 29 October 1947
Playbill (The Browning Version, Harlequinade)	Phoenix Th, 8 Sept 1948	Coronet Th, 12 October 1949
Adventure Story	St James's Th, 17 March 1949	
A Tale of Two Cities (adapt from Dickens, with John Gielgud)	St Brendan's College Dramatic Scy, Clifton, 23 Jan 1950	
Who is Sylvia?	Criterion Th, 24 Oct 1950	
Final Test (tv)	BBC TV 29 July 1951	

The Deep Blue Sea	Duchess Th, 6 March 1952	Morosco Th, 5 Nov 1952
The Sleeping Prince	Phoenix Th, 5 November 1953	Coronet Th, 1 November 1956
Separate Tables (*Table by the Window, Table Number Seven*)	St James's Th, 22 Sept 1954	Music Box Th, 25 Oct 1956
Variation on a Theme	Globe Th, 8 May 1958	
Ross	Theatre Royal, Haymarket, 12 May 1960	Eugene O'Neill Th, 26 Dec 1961
Joie de Vivre (with Robert Stolz, Paul Dehn)	Queen's Th, 14 July 1960	
Heart to Heart (tv)	BBC TV, 6 Dec 1962	
Man and Boy	Queen's Th, 4 Sept 1963	Brooks Atkinson Th, 12 Nov 1963
Ninety Years On (tv)	BBC TV, 29 Nov 1964	
Nelson – a Portrait in Miniature (tv)	Associated Television, 21 March 1966	
All on Her Own (tv) [adapted for stage as *Duologue*]	BBC 2, 25 Sept 1968 King's Head, Feb 1976	
A Bequest to the Nation	Theatre Royal, Haymarket, 23 Sept 1970	
High Summer (tv)	Thames TV, 12 Sept 1972	
In Praise of Love (*After Lydia, Before Dawn*)	Duchess Th, 27 Sept 1973	Morosco Th, 10 Dec 1974
Cause Célèbre (radio)	BBC Radio 4 27 Oct 1975	
Cause Célèbre (stage)	Her Majesty's Th, 4 July 1977	

IN PRAISE OF LOVE

For
BINKIE
and
JOHN

In Praise of Love was first produced at the Duchess Theatre, London, on 27 September 1973, with the following cast:

LYDIA CRUTTWELL   Joan Greenwood
SEBASTIAN CRUTTWELL Donald Sinden
MARK WALTERS   Don Fellows
JOEY CRUTTWELL   Richard Warwick

Director John Dexter
Designer Desmond Healey

Characters

LYDIA CRUTTWELL
SEBASTIAN CRUTTWELL
MARK WALTERS
JOEY CRUTTWELL

Setting: North London
Time: The present

Act One

The CRUTTWELLS' *flat in Islington. We see a small hall,
large living-room and part of a kitchen when the sliding doors
are opened. A staircase – probably put in during conversion –
runs from the living-room: first, up a few steps, to the kitchen
(where the Cruttwells also eat), then turns sharply to lead to
the rooms above. No window is needed, nor fireplace. The
predominant feature of the room is books, for some of which
there is no space but the floor, the book-cases having been
stretched to their limit. There is a book-case even in the
diminutive hall, and on top of that, looking incongruous, a
man's white hat-box which once plainly contained a top hat,
and may still. Other prominent objects are a small table on
which some ordinary black and white chessmen are set out,
plainly for use and not for decoration, a table bearing a tray
of drinks, a sofa and various armchairs. The front door and
hall are at the back and a door, right, leads to* SEBASTIAN's
*work-room. From this is coming the sound of a typewriter
being very intermittently used, with long pauses between short
bouts, usually followed by unmistakable sounds of angry
erasure. It is about six o'clock of a spring evening. The time
is the present.*

LYDIA *lets herself in with a latch-key. A woman of about 50,
very simply dressed, she shows signs of both physical and
mental distress. The physical distress takes the form of utter
exhaustion. She sits on a chair in the hall before she can find
the strength to move into the sitting-room, where she promptly
sits again. She has no parcels to carry, and although the flat is
two flights up from the street (as we will later learn) the long
deep breaths she is taking do not give any impression of
someone who has hurried the stairs. Rather the reverse. Her
mental stress is shown by the slow unblinking stare which
encompasses almost every object in the room, however trivial,*

and by her expression as, her inspection of the room completed, she stares blankly in front of her while she regains her breath.

SEBASTIAN *comes out from his work-room, a cigarette between his lips, an empty glass in his hand, and spectacles over his nose.*

SEBASTIAN. Oh good, darling, you're back. The heating has gone wrong.

LYDIA. Has it? It seems all right in here.

She gets briskly to her feet and feels an ancient radiator.

Yes, it's on.

SEBASTIAN (*at the book-case*). It's icy in my room.

LYDIA goes through the open door of the work-room. SEBASTIAN, left alone, pulls down a book and begins to search for some reference. Vainly. He puts that one on a pile near him and picks another. Same process. LYDIA comes out and quietly takes his glass from his hand.

Oh thank you so much, darling –

She fills up his glass, a procedure she can carry out in her sleep.

LYDIA. You hadn't turned it on.

SEBASTIAN. What on?

LYDIA. The heat.

SEBASTIAN (*deep in a book*). Really?

He says it as if it were a matter of the most breathless interest, a sure sign with him that he hasn't heard a word.

LYDIA comes back with his glass.

Oh thank you, darling. What kept you out so long? Oh, of course, old Doctor Scheister. What did he say?

LYDIA. Schuster. He's very pleased indeed.

SEBASTIAN. What did I tell you? And you got held up by the bus-strike?

LYDIA. Not really. I found a new way on the Tube.

SEBASTIAN (*worried*). Should you have?

LYDIA. Oh, it was quite easy –

SEBASTIAN. I meant isn't it a bit like strike-breaking?

LYDIA. Your social conscience would have preferred I walked?

SEBASTIAN. It's not all that far, is it?

LYDIA. About as far as Fleet Street – to which I notice you've had a hire-car the last three days.

SEBASTIAN. A hire-car is different.

LYDIA. Why?

SEBASTIAN. I charge it to the paper, so it's on their conscience not mine. Good. I've got what I'm looking for – which is a wonder. Darling, our books have got in the most terrible mess again.

He pulls a book out.

Norman Mailer in the poetry section. Why?

Seeing something.

And – I can't believe it – *Tarzan of the Apes*. How did that get there?

LYDIA. You must have reviewed it, some time.

SEBASTIAN. Don't make tasteless jokes . . . Oh yes. I remember. There was a book on Rousseau called *The Noble Savage*, and I had to research.

Throwing her the book.

Well that's for your favourite charity . . . What is it? . . . 'The Little Sisters of the Poor', or do you think it might give those nuns ideas?

LYDIA. Hardly give them. Remind them possibly.

SEBASTIAN (*pointing to the shelf*). Darling, it's an awful muddle. Couldn't Mrs Mackintyre – ?

LYDIA. Mrs Reedy. It hasn't been Mrs MacKintyre for three months.

SEBASTIAN. I call her Mrs MacKintyre.

LYDIA. She's noticed that.

SEBASTIAN *pulls out another book, clicking his teeth.* LYDIA *takes it.*

SEBASTIAN. Well couldn't *she* – ?

LYDIA. No. She isn't, oddly enough, a trained librarian. She isn't a trained anything, come to that. She comes three times a week for two hours a day, never stops eating and costs a bomb.

SEBASTIAN. Is she worth having then?

LYDIA. Yes.

SEBASTIAN. I mean if she costs a bomb –

LYDIA (*loudly*). She's worth having.

SEBASTIAN. A little tetchy this afternoon, are we?

He reaches up and grabs another book.

Plain Talk About Sex – next to *Peter Pan.*

LYDIA (*taking it*). That's mine.

SEBASTIAN. For God's sake, why?

LYDIA. I bought it for a train, sometime.

SEBASTIAN (*taking off his spectacles*). That doesn't answer my question. Darling, I mean, with your early life –

LYDIA. Perhaps it needed a bit of brushing up.

Pause.

SEBASTIAN (*blowing on his glasses, carefully*). A criticism?

LYDIA. No. A comment. Where shall I put these books?

SEBASTIAN. In their proper sections. Where I suggest you might have put the others. You might go through them when you have a little time.

LYDIA. When I have a little time, it will be high on my list.

SEBASTIAN. You're in a stinking mood this evening, aren't you?

LYDIA. Am I?

SEBASTIAN. Was it what I said about your early misadventures?

LYDIA (*smiling*). No, stupid. You of all people have the right to talk about that. I mean thirty years after – nearly thirty – St. George must have occasionally reminded his damsel of the dragon he rescued her from.

SEBASTIAN (*embarrassed*). St George! Really! Anyway St George didn't have several ding-dongs with his damsel before he rescued her –

LYDIA. How do you know he didn't?

SEBASTIAN. Well, he wouldn't have been a saint, would he?

LYDIA. I think it was about what you said about 'criticism'. As if I would –

SEBASTIAN. But you said 'comment'.

LYDIA. There can be good comment as well as bad, can't there?

SEBASTIAN. In theory, yes. In fact, no. Remember, darling, that you're speaking to a critic. You meant something a bit harsh by 'comment'. Oh yes. I know. Now, darling you must realise –

LYDIA. You can't be expected to poke an old skeleton. I know.

SEBASTIAN. Darling, really! That wasn't very – tasteful, was it?

LYDIA. It was your taste. You said it.

SEBASTIAN. Then you shouldn't have remembered it. Not the actual words.

Looking at her.

Did I say skeleton?

LYDIA. Yes, I know. I've put on four pounds in the last four weeks. That's not an invitation – just a fact.

SEBASTIAN (*in 'breathless interest' again*). Have you? Have you really? Put on four pounds? Well, that's splendid – absolutely splendid. I mean, it's marvellous news, isn't it. Marvellous.

He's looking at his book.

LYDIA. You hadn't actually noticed?

SEBASTIAN (*looking up from his book*). Of course I'd noticed. I mean these last few months I've been watching you like a hawk.

Returning to his book.

And I am not so ignorant as not to know that putting on weight is a good sign. Conclusive, in a way –

LYDIA. Well, here's something even more conclusive. I was told by Uncle Constantin to show you this.

She takes a paper from her bag.

It's the result of my last tests.

SEBASTIAN. Oh? When were they taken?

LYDIA. Two weeks ago. That's about average for these days.

SEBASTIAN. Yes, because under the Tories the Health Service personnel were grossly underpaid and even more grossly overworked, so it is hardly unnatural that –

LYDIA. But we're under the other side now.

SEBASTIAN. I am aware of which side we are under, Madam, but, as you know, in my view there is nothing whatever to choose between either of them.

Flourishing the paper.

In a properly organised state-run Health Service –

LYDIA. You'd get the results through by special rocket from the Kremlin, I know. Darling, do read that. It makes nice reading – really it does –

SEBASTIAN. Well, it'll be Greek to me – except that I can read Greek.

LYDIA (*pointing, over his shoulder*). That's my wee-wee test –

SEBASTIAN. Darling, please let's be adult about this. This is your urine test – and this is your faeces test which no doubt you were going you name your 'Ka-Ka' test –

LYDIA. I was. And the others are kidney, liver, heart, etcetera.

Pointing.

Don't read the figures, just the words –

SEBASTIAN (*reading*). Normal, normal, normal, near-normal, normal, normal . . . Sounds like a very dull party –

LYDIA (*eagerly*). And there – under General Remarks –

SEBASTIAN (*reading*). 'Patient's encouraging progress fully maintained. If the results of the biopsy confirm these tests, as early reports suggest, then further monthly tests may be discontinued and the patient may resume her normal life . . . ' The Lab people wrote that?

LYDIA. Of course.

SEBASTIAN (*nodding*). Of course. Oh darling, I *am* glad. Isn't that marvellous for you! – Marvellous. – For me too, of course –

He kisses the top of her head, absently, and picks up a book.

I bet old Schuster is pleased.

LYDIA. Delighted. Imagine, no dieting, no waggon, late nights – anything in the world I like –

SEBASTIAN (*eyebrows raised*). Anything?

LYDIA. Practically anything. He wants me to have a holiday, anyway.

SEBASTIAN. Well, where are we now? – April. Well in a couple of months' time I'll take you to Italy, if there isn't a revolution.

LYDIA. I thought that was what you wanted.

SEBASTIAN (*deep in his book*). Wanted what?

LYDIA. Revolution.

SEBASTIAN (*tetchily*). Darling, not an *Italian* one. It'd be so noisy – tenors blasting off the Internationale in every direction . . . I've lost my place now. Here it is. All right, darling. I'll be about half an hour –

He turns to his door.

LYDIA. You won't.

SEBASTIAN. Won't what?

LYDIA. Be about half an hour. Mark's due here five minutes ago.

SEBASTIAN. Mark? Mark Walters?

LYDIA *nods.*

He's in Hong Kong . . . No, that's right. He's back. I spoke to him yesterday –

LYDIA. And asked him to dinner.

SEBASTIAN. On a *Thursday*? My copy day. I couldn't have –

LYDIA. You did. What's more you asked him to be sure and come an hour early.

SEBASTIAN (*explosively*). Damn and blast! Why didn't you stop me? I remember now. I remember perfectly. You just sat there, with your vapid smile on, and did nothing – *nothing* – there's loyalty –

LYDIA. I thought you must have an easy one this week.

SEBASTIAN. Easy? *Easy*? Two sodding Professors on Shakespeare's imagery taking opposing points of view. Where *is* Mark?

He goes to the telephone.

In that hideous palace of his in Eaton Square – ?

LYDIA. No. The workmen are there, adding something. He's at the Savoy.

Taking the receiver from him.

It's far too late, darling. With the bus-strike and the traffic he must have started an hour ago.

SEBASTIAN. Oh bugger!

LYDIA (*soothingly*). Leave it to me. When he arrives I'll tell him you've got to meet a deadline. He's a writer too.

SEBASTIAN. *Too*? A writer is merely a euphemism, but 'too' is an insult.

LYDIA. Why? I wouldn't mind your selling a million copies before your publication date, and the film rights for half a million, sight unseen –

SEBASTIAN. I see. I see. So that's going to be thrown in my face. My novels sell five thousand and make me about seven hundred pounds in all –

LYDIA. Oh shut up! You don't write novels. I wish you did, but you don't –

SEBASTIAN *opens his mouth to speak.*

Twenty-five years ago you wrote a masterpiece, and followed it up four years later with another –

SEBASTIAN. No. The second was a mess –

LYDIA. It was as good as the first.

SEBASTIAN. It was a mess.

LYDIA. It was only that they all turned on you for not writing *Out of the Night* all over again. And so you gave up and joined the enemy. If you can't beat them, join them, I know, but you did give up a bit soon.

SEBASTIAN. Thank you very much.

LYDIA. My God, if Mark Walters took *his* notices as seriously as you did –

SEBASTIAN. His research staff and his stenographers and the man who writes the descriptive passages between bashes would all be out of a job. And Mark would still be a multi-millionaire. Oh God, the injustice of it all!

He holds out his glass for her to refill. She takes it.

Just take some power-mad tycoon with a permanent hard-on –

LYDIA. They're not all tycoons. His last one was about a
Presidential candidate –

SEBASTIAN. With a permanent hard-on?

LYDIA. Semi-permanent. His son has the permanent one – he
whams it up everything in sight.

SEBASTIAN. A wham a chapter as usual?

LYDIA. Sometimes more, but it averages out. Now the son
meets a lion-tamer –

SEBASTIAN. Don't go on. Being fairly familiar with the
author's 'oeuvre' I can catch the drift.

He looks towards his work-room.

I'll have to work late, that's all – and you know what that
does to my bladder.

LYDIA. You finish now. Mark won't mind. I can delay dinner –

SEBASTIAN *nods gloomily and goes towards his door.*

Oh – talking of novels –

SEBASTIAN. We weren't.

LYDIA. I mean *your* novels. Darling are those notes for a new
novel I came on in there the other day?

Pause.

SEBASTIAN. 'Came on' is good. 'Came on' is very good.
I noticed that they'd been disturbed.

Roaring.

Is there *nothing* I can keep concealed in this house?

LYDIA. Oh – so you *concealed* them, did you? Why?

SEBASTIAN. Because I knew that once you got your X-ray
eyes on them you'd be bouncing up and down, clapping
your little hands and shouting: 'Oh goody, goody, he's
writing a novel!'

LYDIA. Well goody-goody he is.

SEBASTIAN. No. Not necessarily at all. He may well decide
to give it up, because it stinks, or decided that he hasn't got
time for it anyway.

LYDIA. Oh, time isn't important. You can make that –

SEBASTIAN. What utter balls you do talk sometimes –

There is a ring at the front door.

Oh God!

LYDIA. You go in. I'll explain.

SEBASTIAN. No. I'd better say hullo.

*LYDIA opens the front door to MARK. He is in the early
forties, and physically the exact opposite, one would
imagine, of any of his power-mad, randy heroes. He has
a pleasantly mild expression and a weedy physique. He
pants at the mildest physical exertion and is panting now.
He carries two parcels under his arm.*

LYDIA. Mark, darling – this is wonderful –

She throws her arms round his neck.

MARK. Wonderful for me too. Let me get my breath back.
Don't they have elevators in Islington?

SEBASTIAN. No.

MARK. Hell, lifts. As a resident I should remember. Hullo,
Sebastian.

They embrace briefly.

Still murdering literary reputations?

SEBASTIAN. Yours is safe.

MARK. These days no one gives me notices. Even my friends
on the *Cleveland Plain Dealer* who used to find me
'compulsive' now just says 'another Walters!'

SEBASTIAN (*snatching a parcel*). Are these presents?

MARK. You've got Lydia's. This is yours.

LYDIA. Oh Mark, you shouldn't.

SEBASTIAN. Of course he should. It's his duty to redistribute his wealth. Mine rattles.

MARK (*snatching it from him*). Then don't rattle it.

SEBASTIAN. As good as that, eh? I'll open it later, do you mind? I've got a little work to finish off. Lydia forgot it was my copy day –

LYDIA. *He* forgot.

MARK. Look if I'm a nuisance here why don't I take Lydia out for dinner and leave you to work – ?

SEBASTIAN. And how do I get dinner?

MARK. Couldn't you scramble yourself some eggs?

SEBASTIAN. Are you mad?

MARK. Yes, I'm mad. For a moment I was thinking you were a normal husband.

SEBASTIAN. Oh – talking of normal, Mark. Do you remember that little scare we had about the old girl when you were last here? – Not really a scare, of course, but she kept on catching colds and things. You remember how her old throat kept on getting sore?

LYDIA. Less of this old please.

SEBASTIAN. Darling, we must face facts.

LYDIA. I'll face the fact that I'm a year younger than you. Right?

SEBASTIAN. No need to get ugly, darling.

To LYDIA.

Well her doctor, some refugee friend of hers from Riga –

LYDIA. Tallinn –

SEBASTIAN. Put her in rather a flap suddenly. He told her it might be some obscure oriental disease, due to malnutrition –

LYDIA. He didn't say oriental. And he didn't put me in a flap –
I was as calm as ice.

SEBASTIAN. *Cool* as ice, dear. Calm as a mill-pond. And
both of them clichés. But malnutrition, Mark – when you
think how the old girl tucks it away. Eats like a bloody
horse –

LYDIA. I didn't always, you know. We didn't eat like bloody
horses in Estonia between '39 and '46.

SEBASTIAN (*mildly*). Darling, not another refugee story – do
you mind. I'm sure they bore Mark senseless.

To MARK.

Now about this little flap –

MARK. I know about the little flap.

SEBASTIAN. How do you know? You've been in Hong Kong.

LYDIA. There's a postal service even in Hong Kong.

SEBASTIAN (*genuinely surprised*). You write to each other?
How extraordinary! Well, anyway, after a time things got
better and better and today she's had her final clearance, a
piece of paper with 'normal' written all over it. Show it to
him, darling.

LYDIA *hands* MARK *the blood-test. While* MARK *is
reading:*

What's more she's put on ten pounds.

LYDIA. Four. Three really.

MARK. Well, that's great, Lydia.

He hands it to her. She puts it on a table.

SEBASTIAN. You saw that note at the end telling her to piss
off and not bother them any more? She shouldn't have
written to you, Mark, and bothered you.

MARK. I like being bothered.

SEBASTIAN. I don't write and tell you about my bladder
trouble, do I?

MARK. No.

Politely.

How is your bladder trouble?

SEBASTIAN. Absolutely terrible. Sometimes I sit in there, screaming.

MARK. Screaming what?

SEBASTIAN. For someone to care. You look terrible.

MARK. I know. I always do.

SEBASTIAN. Why don't you look like your heroes?

MARK. If I did I'd write about heroes who looked like me, and I wouldn't sell.

SEBASTIAN (*having laughed*). I often think if you'd had any education you might actually write.

MARK. If I'd had any education I'd know I couldn't.

SEBASTIAN (*kissing his cheek*). I love you a little, do you know that?

(*To* LYDIA.) Darling, fill this up, would you, and then get Mark a drink.

LYDIA *takes his glass again.*

MARK. How's Joey?

LYDIA (*eagerly*). Oh he's doing wonderfully well, Mark.

SEBASTIAN. Wonderfully well? He has an unpaid job at the headquarters of a crypto-fascist political organisation called the Liberal Party.

MARK. Jesus! You mean the party that Gladstone was once head of?

SEBASTIAN (*pronouncing correctly, whereas* MARK *pronounced it to rhyme with 'bone'*). Gladstone. *Gladstone* is the name of a hotel in New York, isn't it?

MARK. No, seriously. That party that got all those votes in the last election – is *that* crypto-fascist?

LYDIA. That was a little joke, Mark.

SEBASTIAN. It was *not* a little joke. The modern Liberal
Party is a vote-splitting organisation carefully designed to
keep the Establishment in power under cosy left-wing
labels, and the real Left forever out. And moreover, there is
little doubt that the whole movement is clandestinely
backed by South African gold –

LYDIA (*to* MARK *who looks confused*). That was another
little joke . . . Oh Mark, don't you think it's wonderful Joey
getting that job all by himself?

SEBASTIAN. Unpaid.

LYDIA. Only now. After the bye-election they're going to pay
him.

SEBASTIAN. Thirty pieces of silver, I should think.

MARK (*still at sea*). Bye-election?

Pause.

SEBASTIAN. How long have you lived in England, Mark?

MARK. Well, now, let's see. I came over first for the English
publication of *The Naked Truth,* or was it *Pride of
Possession*, so that would be –

SEBASTIAN. Don't let's see. I should never have brought it
up. A bye-election is –

MARK (*in the nick of time*). – when a Member of Parliament
dies and they elect his successor. We have the same thing in
the States –

SEBASTIAN. And what do they call them there?

Pause.

MARK. Bye-elections, I guess.

SEBASTIAN (*at length*). Christ. Do you read nothing but
Terry and the Pirates?

MARK. It's just that with us bye-elections aren't all that
important. Are they here?

SEBASTIAN. In your benighted country you have elections every two years: in our even more benighted one we have ours every five – well, usually that is. With us a bye-election is an authentic indication of what the voters are thinking about government policies. – Take this bye-election at East Worsley, for instance, where my son is currently working for the Liberals.

The thought of it overcomes him.

The Liberals, Mark! Helping to split the Left and let the Tories in! . . . My own son, Mark – My own son!

MARK. Too bad. Go on.

SEBASTIAN. Well it's a safe Labour seat. Majority never fallen below ten thousand. But with a *Liberal* candidate canvassed for by Joey and by hundreds of other little Joeys, with their clean hair, winning smiles, fetching little turtle-necks, unstained little leather jackets – No. The thought is too awful to be borne – My own son, Mark – my own son – helping the enemy . . . Perhaps putting a Tory in –

LYDIA. Isn't it awful.

After a pause – brightly.

You know he's earned three hundred pounds, Mark, for a television play he's written. Isn't that marvellous?

She gives SEBASTIAN *his drink.*

SEBASTIAN. The BBC2 series for which this piece of pseudo-Kafka crap was written, Mark, happens to be limited to plays by authors under twenty-one –

LYDIA. It's still an achievement – and you ought to be proud.

SEBASTIAN. Oh I am, very.

He sips his drink.

A touch too much water, darling.

LYDIA *angrily snatches the drink back.*

MARK. When's this play being done?

LYDIA Tomorrow at 7.30.

MARK. I'll try and get to watch.

SEBASTIAN (*in a murmur*). Don't.

LYDIA. You wouldn't come and watch it here with us, would you?

She brings the drink back to SEBASTIAN *having added whisky.*

SEBASTIAN. Darling, what a thing to ask the poor man!

LYDIA. It's only he could see Joey too. He's coming up from his bye-election especially to watch it with us. Don't you think that's rather sweet of him, when he could have seen it with his friends?

SEBASTIAN. I think it's wise. He knows we've got to like it.

LYDIA. Damn you, damn you!

She begins to switch lights on.

SEBASTIAN. Forgive her, Mark. She's been a bit hysterical lately.

LYDIA. Go and work.

SEBASTIAN (*soothingly*). Yes, darling, I'm just going.

SEBASTIAN *goes to his door.*

LYDIA. Would you, Mark? I know it's an awful thing to ask but Joey would be thrilled out of his mind.

SEBASTIAN. Out of his what?

MARK. I'd love to.

SEBASTIAN. Good God.

He goes out.

MARK *faces* LYDIA. *There is a pause.*

MARK. Tell me please that I've come for no reason.

LYDIA. You've come, Marcus, and I'm eternally grateful.

MARK. What you told me in your last letter is true?

LYDIA. Well, while there's life and Marcus Waldt –

Holding him.

– darling, darling Marcus Waldt – there must be hope –

MARK. You're goddamn right there's hope.

He studies the tests.

LYDIA *goes to the drink table. She pours herself a drink.*

LYDIA. I'm going to give myself a drink. First in six months. Sure you won't have one?

MARK. Sure.

Indicating the papers.

These reports are phoney. Is that what you're trying to tell me?

LYDIA. Yes.

MARK. How do you know?

LYDIA. I know Uncle Constantin's typewriter. His Ss and Es don't work.

MARK. Uncle Constantin?

LYDIA. The one I wrote you about.

MARK. Oh. And he typed them?

LYDIA. Yes.

MARK. Why?

LYDIA. A kind of reassuring word sent out to a friend in need.

A shade wearily.

But not even darling Uncle Constantin could fake or forge the figures on official laboratory paper. Those figures are worse than last month's – and a great deal worse than the month's before.

MARK. How do you know?

LYDIA. Oh, I get to see them.

MARK. How do you get to see them?

LYDIA. I pinch them, memorise the figures, and then put them back in Uncle Constantin's desk, exactly as they were.

MARK. I don't believe that.

LYDIA. Don't. It doesn't matter –

MARK. It does.

Pause.

LYDIA. I'm sorry, Marcus. Yes, it does. Well, you mustn't forget that in between bouts of concentration camps I did serve a little time in Estonian Resistance – when there *was* any Estonian Resistance – With three invasions, from different sides, it wasn't too easy –

MARK (*harshly*). I know all that. Come to the point.

Pause.

LYDIA. I'm sorry. Refugee stories. They bore you senseless –

MARK. They don't and you know it. But please come to the point.

LYDIA. Well, I learnt a little about memorising figures. If you train yourself to do that at eighteen, you don't forget the knack – never mind. You also learn to rifle desks quickly, knowing which are the operative drawers. – Well, Uncle Constantin wouldn't have made a very high rank in the Gestapo – poor lamb – or the KGB – You see each time I go to him I have to spend a penny for a wee-wee – sorry, *urine* test – and I tell him I can't do it with someone in the room, even behind a screen. So he discreetly disappears and I'm into his desk the way I did with that Russian General, remember, I told you.

MARK. Yes. Go on.

LYDIA. There's nothing to go on about. You see I know what they've all been looking for these last six months –

MARK. How?

LYDIA. By listening – Mainly to student doctors. They're always around at these tests, with their young eager, pretty faces – Well, not always pretty – but eager anyway. I'd address them in fluent Estonian which somehow seemed to give them the idea that I didn't speak English. So they, sometimes, did between themselves. And that particular word came to stick out.

MARK. Poly – Arteritis?

LYDIA. Darling Marcus – you really must care a bit! You've even learnt the word.

MARK. Don't be coy.

He takes out a note-book and begins comparing the figures in the tests sheets which he is holding with others in his notebook.

LYDIA. That hurt. – Yes, I *am* being. I'm sorry. I'm getting myself another drink –

MARK (*sharply*). Allowed it?

LYDIA. Encouraged, Marcus, encouraged.

She takes a sip.

Oh God, how horrible American Vodka is! – Still it's better than prune juice.

After another sip.

Just better – What are you doing?

MARK. The minute I read your letter I put my best researcher on to –

LYDIA. Oh Marcus, I do love you.

MARK (*absently*). And I love you too. Do you happen to know your blood pressure?

LYDIA. With my resistance training, do you think I can't read upside down?

MARK. What is it?

LYDIA. High.

MARK. How high?

LYDIA. Very.

MARK. How long has it stayed that way?

Pause.

LYDIA. Your researcher's done his work well, hasn't he? Well I've done some researching too. For far too long to give me any kind of a chance.

MARK (*violently*). Don't talk that way!

LYDIA (*quietly*). I will, if I want to. To you, anyway. That's what you're here for, Marcus. Cheers!

MARK. Lydia, if you have got this thing, it's bad. It's even very bad. But – look – it's not necessarily fatal –

Pause.

LYDIA. Your researcher and I seem to have been reading different books. Of course it takes time. It could even take two years.

She finishes her vodka.

Hell – it doesn't even taste like vodka. Still – who's caring what it tastes like?

She pours another.

It's what it does that matters. And what it does is good. So here's to two years –

MARK. Listen. This I do know. There can be no certain diagnosis until there's been a biopsy. You know that, don't you?

LYDIA. Yes.

After drinking.

There's been a biopsy.

MARK (*triumphantly tapping the tests*). But the result isn't through. It says so here –

LYDIA. It says a lot of things there.

MARK. Is the result through?

LYDIA. No. Not officially.

MARK. Well, then –

LYDIA. Have you forgotten 'Lydia, Heroine of the Glorious
    Estonian Resistance'? – Heroine is funny. Me and two small
    boys, none of us lasting more than six weeks – But still,
    who needs the written result when you can get the verbal
    one more quickly and more easily. – That was in our
    manual – Uncle Constantin's nurse is Scandinavian, you
    see. Accent very like mine. So today I call the hospital,
    get the consultant's secretary, say Doctor Schuster needs
    a verbal report and couldn't speak himself as the patient's
    in his consulting-room at that moment. She swallowed it
    like a nice Scandinavian lamb. Said she'd look it up –

MARK. You called from the doctor's office?

LYDIA. No. In a call-box, scared to death it would sound off
    too soon. It didn't. She came back. 'Mrs Lydia Cruttwell.
    Poly-arteritis. Positive.' Very brisk voice. Very Swedish –
    very – healthy-sounding. So there you are. Now you'll have
    that drink?

MARK. Yes.

> LYDIA *gets it. Pause. He sips his drink.* LYDIA *sits beside
> him.*

And he doesn't know a thing?

LYDIA. No.

MARK. Shouldn't you have let him know?

LYDIA. No.

> *After a pause.*

How was Hong Kong?

MARK. What I expected.

LYDIA. Susie Wongs everywhere?

MARK. Sammy Wongs more. – Is that funny?

LYDIA. No.

MARK. I'll lose it.

Toward door.

He should know.

LYDIA (*she kisses his cheek*). And just what do I tell him?

MARK. The truth for Christ's sake! Isn't the truth what you tell your husband?

LYDIA. Not this husband.

MARK. But he'll have to be told sometime.

LYDIA. When the ambulance comes. Not before. Perhaps not even then.

Pause.

MARK. Listen, he could *resent* your not telling him, you know that?

LYDIA. Oh yes, he could. He probably will. In fact he certainly will –

MARK. Then why – ?

LYDIA. Because I won't bore him, I love him too much for that. Marcus, don't let's fool ourselves – is there any surer way of boring our nearest and dearest than by getting ourselves a long slow terminal illness?

MARK. But isn't that just what our nearest and dearest are for?

LYDIA. You are. And don't *you* worry – I'll bore *you* good and proper before I'm through – Is that correct idiom, 'good and proper'? Or should it be 'well and properly'?

MARK. Good and proper will do.

LYDIA. But Sebastian isn't you –

MARK. You got a point there.

LYDIA. I mean he's so bad at being bored. You must have noticed that –

MARK. I've noticed it.

LYDIA. Of course if I *had* told him he'd have been quite upset –
perhaps even very upset – for a week or so, and he'd have
remembered his manners too. Manners Makyth Man. That's
the motto of his old school, Winchester. 'Don't tire yourself,
old girl. just lie there. I'll get you your tea.'

She laughs.

Oh God, just to hear that I sometimes wish I *had* told him.
But not for two years, Mark. Two years!

She touches wood surreptitiously.

No, Marcus, I've chosen this way, and it's the best way. The
best for me, as well as for him. I promise you.

Pause.

MARK. God damn it, why do you look so well?

LYDIA. Cortisone! Lashings of cortisone! What Uncle
Constantin calls my vitamin pills. Which reminds me.

*She takes a bottle from her bag, and shakes two into her
hand.*

Two six times a day now. It was two four times a day.

She swallows two.

I don't know whether that's a good sign or a bad sign – Bad,
I suppose, but who cares? . . . Cortisone's a marvellous
drug, Marcus. It makes one feel sixteen. They dope
racehorses with it –

MARK (*taking the bottle from her*). It doesn't say cortisone.

LYDIA. Of course it doesn't. Uncle Constantin's far too cute
for that. He has them specially labelled –

MARK. Then how do you know they're cortisone?

LYDIA. Heroine of the Estonian Resistance at English chemist –
Heavy Baltic accent – Could you Miss, helping me please?
These pills am I finding in old bottle – I am thinking they
are aspirin – are they so being? . . . A little wait, then . . .

Not aspirin? Cortisone? . . . Powerful drug? Then down the loo-loo am I putting them – instantly . . .

Her voice is beginning to quaver. She ends the speech in near tears, her head on his chest.

You're supposed to be laughing –

MARK. I guess so.

LYDIA. Oh Marcus, are you angry with me for pulling you half across the globe just to hear me whining – Not much of a Heroine am I? – The thing is I had to tell someone. It couldn't be Sebastian, so it had to be you – which is a song, I think.

MARK. Want me to sing it?

LYDIA. Later. Oh Marcus, I'm so happy to see you. Thank you for coming.

MARK. You said that already.

LYDIA. Yes, I did, didn't I? I don't know why it is that you're the only real friend I've got.

MARK. Nor do I.

LYDIA. It must be something to do with your being Lithuanian –

MARK. I'm not Lithuanian, I'm American. And you're British . . .

LYDIA. I mean, Baltic blood.

MARK. In my case more Jewish than Baltic –

LYDIA. No need to boast. I had a Jewish grandfather, remember.

MARK. You didn't even know that until the Nazis came –

LYDIA. I knew it then all right.

She suppresses a shiver.

No, the English aren't easy to make friends from – and, of course, as a refugee in 1945 I started off on the wrong foot.

She laughs reminiscently.

A few days after I got here, when I was delirious with joy, and loving England and everything English –

MARK. Not their cabbage?

LYDIA. Even their cabbage – Sebastian asked about ten or twelve of his best friends round to meet me.

MARK. Before the wedding?

LYDIA. No, after. We got married in Berlin. I thought you knew that –

Remembering something.

No, you didn't, and there's a good reason why you didn't – why nobody does – Back to Sebastian's party. Do you know, Mark, the party started at nine and at eleven there was no one left. No one at all. I'd bored the whole lot out into the night.

MARK. Refugee stories?

LYDIA (*indignantly*). I didn't know they were forbidden! I mean, people that night asked me politely about what it had been like being invaded alternately by the Russians, then by the Germans and then by the Russians again over six years – and like a bloody idiot I went and told them. All of them. Finally, they were round me in a circle, looking at me so politely – you know those polite English looks – Oh God, how I hate polite English looks . . . !

MARK. I hate politeness.

LYDIA (*aggressively*). You don't. You're the politest man I know –

MARK. Yeh, but I don't look it.

LYDIA. True. Sebastian's friends did. Glassy-eyed from boredom, of course, but I didn't see that. Sebastian did and tried to stop me, but I wasn't to be stopped. I told them all about myself – All!

MARK. Even the Russian General?

LYDIA. You bet, the Russian General . . . You see the one thing I was so sure about the English, was that they all had a sense of humour . . . Famous for it . . . So when I told them that a Russian General had selected me from a Labour Camp to be his personal driver because he liked my 'Body-work', oh how I thought they'd roar –

MARK. Not a titter?

LYDIA. Not a smirk.

MARK. Well there wouldn't be, would there? It's a terrible joke.

LYDIA (*indignantly*). It was the best I could manage in the circumstances –

A pause.

Oh, those glassy stares! – Oh God, and how angry Sebastian was!

Imitating him.

'You see, my darling girl, it isn't quite done over here to parade your emotions so publicly. We as a race, on the whole prefer to – *understate*. Do you understand, my darling?' – I was guilty of bad form, especially as, I think I did, I cried a bit when I told them . . . Oh damn the English! Sometimes I think that their bad form doesn't just lie in revealing their emotions, it's in having any at all. Do you like the English?

MARK. I don't quite dig them, of course, but who does?

LYDIA (*sadly*). Who does? – Who does?

MARK. Still I like their country, so I live in it rather than mine.

Indicating his glass.

May I?

LYDIA. Yes – and get me another vodka.

MARK (*doubtfully*). Should you? After all you've already had –

LYDIA. Why not?

MARK (*giving her her drink*). I can think of reasons.

LYDIA. Don't.

MARK. O.K. I won't.

Facing her.

Why didn't I know you got married in Berlin?

Pause.

LYDIA. I said I couldn't tell you that.

MARK. But you *can* tell me you're dying.

LYDIA (*angrily*). Who said anything about dying? – Eighteen months to two years – why, it's a life-time.

MARK *laughs.* LYDIA *glares at him angrily.*

Why didn't you stay in Hong Kong?

MARK. Because you asked me to come here.

Pause.

LYDIA. What is so important about where I got married?

MARK. I don't know, but if you've kept it a secret from me for twenty-five years, it's important. So I should know. Now, I mean.

Pause.

LYDIA. Inquisitor!

MARK. The Grand.

Pause.

LYDIA. It's only feminine pride that's stopped me telling you, that's all –

MARK (*surprised*). Bun in the oven?

LYDIA (*outraged*). No! And that's a revolting expression. Wherever did you learn it?

MARK. From a Susie Wong. They all speak English slang –

LYDIA. You lead a shocking life –

MARK. I wish it shocked me.

Pause.

LYDIA. Sebastian married me in Berlin because that was the
only way he could marry me at all. I was still a Russian
citizen, Estonia having vanished into Russia. Sebastian was
a British Intelligence Officer, with contacts. In fact I'm not
at all sure that Marshall Zhukov didn't have a hand in it
somewhere.

Boldly, after a pause.

Sebastian never took me for better, for worse, Mark – in
sickness and in health to love and cherish, till death do us
part. He took me for one reason only: to give me a British
passport.

Pause.

MARK. Other reasons too, surely?

LYDIA. Two, if you like. That night I first met him and later
nights too – I made him enjoy going to bed with me –
I'd learnt how to by then. You see – even with the visiting
Politburo. Besides a British Junior Officer was – was – well
quite a change from some of those very Senior Russians –
and for the first time I – oh dear – I'd say I enjoyed my
work! – Then my funny English made him laugh that night,
and other nights, and I think my being a kind of slave – we
weren't paid, you know – just bed and board – that shocked
him, coming from his friends, the Russians. So he decided
to rescue me – Poor Sebastian! It was much more of a job
than he'd thought, but he sticks to things once he's decided,
and I finally ended up with a passport made out to Mrs
Sebastian Cruttwell, with a British Occupation Authority
Stamp all over it . . . We must have had some kind of
wedding, I suppose, but I can't remember it. I can only
remember Sebastian roaring at some British Chaplain that
he'd be buggered if he'd say 'Obey'. He thought that was
his line, you see –

MARK. But I imagine he made no objection when he found
out that it was yours?

LYDIA. Asked for a repetition. Our agreement – kind of unspoken – was that once in England we'd get ourselves a divorce. But he was writing a novel then, and I was typing it, and collecting material, and generally making myself useful . . . Too useful to be got rid of! – deliberately, Mark, deliberately. You see – well you've always known – I was in love with him – always have been, in spite of –

Suddenly angry with him.

All right, I might have gone away with you when you asked me. I didn't lie to you. I nearly did go away with you.

MARK. Not very nearly, I think.

LYDIA (*angry again*). Oh you don't know how nearly. You don't know what being married to a Sebastian is like –

MARK. Happily, I don't.

LYDIA. Then it had been only for three years. Now it's twenty-eight. Twenty-eight years! Jesus!

MARK. Jesus indeed.

LYDIA. And after Joey appeared, then there was no longer any question . . .

She stops short.

Oh damn it! Why did I mention Joey? Now I've gone and made myself cry –

She sobs quietly on his breast.

MARK. Does Joey know?

LYDIA (*fiercely*). Of course he doesn't. And he mustn't. Like Sebastian, he mustn't – oh God. Joey!

Pause.

MARK. Yes, I'm glad I'm here. I'm glad you've got somebody around.

He holds her in a light embrace. SEBASTIAN *puts his head round the door.*

SEBASTIAN. Darling, my special reading light doesn't go on.

Neither MARK *nor* LYDIA *show any embarrassment at their intimate attitude.*

Darling, I said my special reading light –

LYDIA. I heard you. What's the matter with it?

SEBASTIAN (*simply and reasonably*). It doesn't go on.

LYDIA. Probably the bulb.

She goes past him into the room.

SEBASTIAN. Do forgive me, Mark. Just two more sentences. You haven't been too bored, I hope.

MARK. Not at all. What are you writing on this week?

SEBASTIAN. That complacent old burgher of Stratford-on-Avon. God, he's so maddening. With his worship of the Establishment he makes nonsense of everything we write, don't you think?

MARK. *We*?

SEBASTIAN (*appalled*). Are you a *Republican*?

MARK (*hastily*). Gee no. I'm a Democrat –

SEBASTIAN. Well Shakespeare *must* infuriate people like us who passionately believe that no man can write well whose heart isn't in the right place.

MARK. Meaning the left place?

SEBASTIAN (*feeling his heart*). Which is where the heart is. Thank you, Mark. I might use that as my pay-off.

LYDIA *appears.*

Well?

LYDIA. It wasn't plugged in.

SEBASTIAN. Who unplugged it? Mrs Macreedy?

LYDIA. Mrs Reedy. Probably she did.

SEBASTIAN. You must speak to her, darling. Set up the chessmen, Mark.

He goes into his room. There is a pause.

MARK. Now who on earth is going to look after him, if –

LYDIA. Say 'when', Mark. Get used to it, please.

MARK (*stubbornly*). I'm not saying 'when', Lydia. I'm sorry. Someone's got to keep a little hope going around here. You seemed to have resigned yourself to black despair –

LYDIA. Black despair! *Me*! Really, Mark. I left that behind in Bentinck Strasse. You don't think I'm scared of dying, do you?

MARK. I think you've resigned yourself to it far too soon. You're not fighting, Lydia –

LYDIA. What is there to fight? If you've got it, it kills you – and that's that. But if my books are right it kills you quite gently – 'To cease upon the midnight with no pain'. Can't you well-fed, uninvaded Americans understand how many millions of us in Europe during those years longed for just that – and didn't get it? – Black despair! Me? I'm insulted –

MARK. All right, all right. I'd sooner not talk about it too much, if you don't mind.

He pulls one of his parcels out and begins to open it.

LYDIA. Well, we've got to talk about it a little or you're not going to be much of a help, are you?

MARK. O.K., but not now. Do you mind?

LYDIA. Just one thing more. You asked a question and I've got to answer it.

MARK is taking out a set of very beautiful, carved, Chinese chessmen, in red and white, and is methodically replacing the black and white pieces with them on the table in the corner. LYDIA, obsessed with her problem, has not yet noticed what he is unobtrusively doing.

Who's going to look after that one.

She thumbs at SEBASTIAN's door.

When *I* can't any more. Well I've an idea –

MARK. I suppose he couldn't just look after himself?

LYDIA. Are you mad?

MARK. Hasn't he ever *had* to? Surely in the war –

LYDIA. Commission in Army Intelligence at once, and with a batman. Knowing him, probably two. What are you doing over there?

MARK. Don't look yet. How does he reconcile all that with his Marxism?

LYDIA. Surprisingly easily. No, I've got an idea. There's a girl called Prunella Larkin – a journalist, who's mad about him, and I gather rather his form too, mentally *and* physically. Anyway he's been seeing an awful lot of her recently. In fact I think for the last three months they've been having a thing –

MARK. You don't say. How do you know it's a thing?

LYDIA. Well he's not a master of subterfuge. He takes this Larkin out to dinner – a little business chat, you know, darling – and later gets caught in the rain when there isn't any, and stays the night with his Editor who sends him a postcard the next day from Tangier. You know the form.

MARK. Who better? Only my wives didn't go to that much trouble. They just slept around and when I asked who with – it was mental cruelty.

LYDIA. Now the doctor says I must have a holiday. Will you take me away for ten days?

MARK. Sure. Where?

LYDIA. Brighton's nice –

MARK. Monte Carlo's nicer. What's this to do with Miss Larkin?

LYDIA. Mrs Larkin, divorced. Well when I tell him I'm going off with you for ten days, he'll say: 'Yes, that's fine for you darling – but who the hell is going to look after *me*?' Wouldn't you say that's likely?

MARK. I'd say it's goddam certain. So?

LYDIA. So I'll say: 'What about that nice girl Prunella you're always talking about – The one that's so intelligent, and bright and admires your writing so much . . . I wonder if *she'd* move in here, and look after you? – or maybe you could move in with her?' – He'll jump at it, of course. So if their ten days together are a success – well, I can make my plans for the future accordingly. I mean I'll have found my replacement, won't I?

Pause.

MARK. What exactly would be those plans?

LYDIA. Well, I could maybe fade into the background a bit sooner than I needed – knowing at least that someone is plugging in his reading lamp . . . And I'd be able to put my feet up and read Agatha Christie –

Another pause.

Well? Don't you think it's a clever idea?

MARK. I can only repeat what Sebastian so often says to you: you are an extraordinary woman. All right. Now you can look.

He carries the completed table over to the centre of the room. LYDIA *looks in wonder.*

LYDIA (*picking up a piece*). Oh but these are exquisite.

MARK. Chinese. Nothing very grand. Modern.

LYDIA. But they're beautiful. He'll adore them. My God, if his is as good as that, I'm going to open mine.

She snatches up the remaining parcel and begins furiously to unwrap it.

MARK. Listen – if that doesn't suit –

LYDIA *has managed to open the parcel which is a box and peers inside, past tissue paper. Then she closes the box.*

LYDIA. No. Take it back.

MARK. Lydia.

LYDIA. Take it back this instant.

*But she holds on to it firmly. There is a pause. Then,
gathering strength, she whisks out a silver mink wrap.
She gazes at it lovingly.*

I said – take it back.

MARK. I heard you.

*He takes the wrap from her and holds it out for her to slip
into. She does so.*

LYDIA. I didn't mean a word of what I said just now. I think
you're an absolute horror.

MARK. Yes.

LYDIA. Flaunting your wealth, showing girls what they've
missed by not divorcing their husbands and marrying you.

*She looks at herself from every angle in the mirror. Then she
gives him a passionate embrace. Finally she takes his empty
glass.*

You can't just say thank you for mink, can you? I'll say it
in Estonian. It sounds better. Tanan vaga. If you think I'm
ever going to take this off, you're crazy. Marcus, don't
redistribute your wealth quite so much, please. If I'd been
your wife I wouldn't have let you give mink coats to old
lady friends –

She gives him his glass.

MARK. Well, maybe I sensed this was special.

LYDIA. Special it was. Thank you, dear Marcus.

She embraces him again. SEBASTIAN *comes in.*

SEBASTIAN. Have you two nothing better to do? You're not
even giving the poor man a chance to smoke.

LYDIA. I haven't seen him for six months.

SEBASTIAN. Nor have I. Nor has anyone. Darling, that lovely
patent folding table of yours doesn't fold –

LYDIA (*looking in the room*). Well, of course, it doesn't if you leave the typewriter on it.

She flaunts her wrap in front of his eyes, to no effect whatever. Crossly she goes into the work-room.

SEBASTIAN (*very half-heartedly after her*). Oh darling – do let me –

He takes half a step to the work-room, and three or four full and determined steps over to the drink tray.

MARK. Finished?

SEBASTIAN. More or less. I've fixed both the Professors, and the Swan is sunk in his own Avon without a trace.

MARK. Never to rise again?

SEBASTIAN. Ay. There's the rub. One has to admit that the bloody old honours-hunting bourgeois could write. William Shakespeare, Gent. Hard to forgive him for that. It should have stamped him a forgettable nonentity for the rest of creation. Instead of which –

MARK. Didn't you get something?

SEBASTIAN. An OBE.

With rage.

Lydia forced me into that. She staged a sit-down strike.

MARK. Isn't an OBE what's called an honour?

SEBASTIAN. I would rather not speak of it, if you please.

He slips into the chair opposite MARK, *facing him across the chessmen. He picks up a white pawn in one hand, and a red one in the other.*

Now, are you prepared for your usual thrashing?

MARK *taps his left hand.* SEBASTIAN *opens it, revealing a red pawn.*

Good. There is no question at all that I am better playing red than – Red?

He picks up his pawn again, feels it lovingly and then stares at the whole board. Then without a word he gets up, crosses to MARK *and gives him a full, fervent kiss on the mouth.*

I passionately adore you, and am prepared to live with you for the rest of my life.

He picks up more pieces to feel them.

What is more I take everything back that I've ever written about your novels.

MARK. You've never written anything about my novels.

SEBASTIAN. Your next one will get my whole three columns –

MARK. I think I'd rather have a kiss.

SEBASTIAN. Nonsense. I can always find something to praise. Your un-put-down-ability . . . rattling good yarn . . . every story tells a picture.

To himself.

That's rather good. I must remember that.

MARK *moves a piece.*

Pawn to *Queen* four? What's the matter? You've got bored with pawn to King four?

SEBASTIAN *answers the move appropriately.*

MARK. I've been studying Fischer-Spassky.

SEBASTIAN. You mean you've had your research staff study Fischer-Spassky.

MARK. Touché. You know something. I'd give a million bucks to write one novel a tenth as good as your *Out of the Night.*

SEBASTIAN. So would I. Only I haven't a million bucks.

Picking up his King and Queen to fondle them.

These are marvellous. Of course you can't tell the King from the Queen, but when can you these days?

MARK. Are you never going to try another novel?

SEBASTIAN. That'd be telling.

MARK. Good. That means yes.

SEBASTIAN. No. You said 'try'. I've got to be *moved*, Mark. The war did move me and that novel was good. It wasn't Tolstoy like some idiots said, but it was good. The Peace didn't stir the juices, and that novel was bad.

MARK. No.

SEBASTIAN (*belligerently*). Listen, who's the critic here?

MARK. Sorry.

SEBASTIAN. But I'm not beyond hope about the next – if I do it. Ah.

Referring to the game.

The Queen's gambit. I thought you'd grown out of that –

MARK. I've got a new variation –

SEBASTIAN. You'll need it. My reply to the Queen's gambit makes strong men quake –

He takes a central pawn.

Queen's gambit – *accepted.*

MARK. You're not supposed to do that.

LYDIA *comes in unobserved.*

SEBASTIAN. Why not?

MARK. It'll weaken your central pawn position later –

SEBASTIAN (*complacently*). Let it. Let it. Meanwhile you're a pawn down.

To LYDIA *who is moving about, ostentatiously showing off her wrap.*

Darling, can you leave the ashtrays till later? It's a bit distracting, all that moving about.

LYDIA *stands still with a sigh.*

Oh, by the way – do you see what Mark's given me?

LYDIA. I'm trying to show you what Mark's given me.

SEBASTIAN (*looking up at her*). Oh, what?

After a pause.

Oh, that.

Another pause. To MARK.

What fur exactly is that?

LYDIA (*explosively*). Don't tell him!

Savagely.

Dyed rabbit.

SEBASTIAN. Mink? I see.

Pause.

Very nice.

Pause.

Isn't that light shade just a bit – forgive me, darling – on the young side – ?

Before he has finished LYDIA *has slipped the wrap off and has swung it at his head, disturbing several chess pieces. Outraged.*

Darling, really. These are valuable –

He and MARK *pick up the pieces.* LYDIA *goes to sit down in a sulk, hand on fist, staring at her husband with hatred.*

I'd just moved Pawn to King three.

Holding a pawn.

Superb workmanship.

He allows MARK *to re-arrange the board.*

Where did you get them?

MARK. Hong Kong.

SEBASTIAN. Of course.

A horrifying thought strikes him.

Oh Mark, I may have to give them back. All that sweated labour –

MARK. Imported from Pekin.

SEBASTIAN (*with a deep sigh of relief*). Ah. Good.

MARK. It's all right if they sweat in Pekin?

SEBASTIAN. They don't sweat in Pekin.

MARK. Or they'd be arrested.

SEBASTIAN. Please don't make cheap jokes like that, do you mind? Now. Your move.

They have re-arranged the board. LYDIA, *after a questioning glance at* MARK, *fills up her own glass.*

LYDIA. Sebastian, Mark wants to take me down to Monte Carlo for ten days or so –

SEBASTIAN. What for?

LYDIA. A holiday. A rest – like the doctor said –

SEBASTIAN. Well, can't you have a rest here?

LYDIA. Since you ask – no. Unless you go to Monte Carlo instead.

SEBASTIAN. Well that might be an idea. I doubt if my Editor would scream with joy though, seeing he's away too.

LYDIA. In Tangier.

SEBASTIAN. Yes. How did you know? Well, can you get Mrs Macreedy to come in every day?

LYDIA. Not a chance.

SEBASTIAN. Just as well. It'd be very expensive.

LYDIA. But I've got a better idea. I haven't asked her, but I think I might just get Prunella to look after you.

SEBASTIAN. Prunella? Prunella Larkin?

LYDIA. Yes. Just for that little time.

Pause.

SEBASTIAN. There is no such thing as a little time with Prunella Larkin. An hour is an eternity. Ten days – ten *consecutive* days with her and I'd be a gibbering lunatic.

LYDIA (*not displeased*). Oh. It's just that you did seem to have been seeing quite a lot of her recently –

Pause.

SEBASTIAN (*carefully*). Mrs Larkin and I do, I grant, have certain interests in common, but they are interests that can usually be shared in well under thirty minutes of fairly *concentrated converse*. If after those brief encounters I should choose not to plod back to Islington but to sleep in my Editor's flat, to which I have a key, that is a matter for my conscience but not for your prurient suspicions. If you insist on skipping off on this extravagant jaunt, I shall go to the Savoy and send the bill in to Mark. If he doesn't pay I shall sell these chessmen. Now, does that settle the matter?

LYDIA (*a shade breathlessly*). Yes. Oh yes. Oh yes, it does.

SEBASTIAN. Good.

Gravely.

Your move, Mark.

LYDIA *suddenly bursts into a peal of slightly drunken laughter and kisses his head.*

Darling, please. This game needs concentration. Bobby Fischer won't have a camera click ten yards away – much less a hyena screeching tipsily in his ear.

LYDIA. Sorry. I was trying to kiss you.

SEBASTIAN. There is a time and a place.

LYDIA. Yes. I know both.

Trying to be very silent, she puts down her glass, fumbles in her bag and takes out two pills from the familiar bottle. In doing so she knocks a glass over.

SEBASTIAN. Darling, go and cook dinner.

LYDIA. Yes.

She swallows the pills with a sip of vodka. MARK *sees her.*

MARK (*sharply*). You've already had two of those –

LYDIA. Yes, but I missed two after lunch.

SEBASTIAN. What's she had two of?

LYDIA. My tonic pills.

SEBASTIAN (*deep in thought*). Oh yes, those iron things. Very good for her, Mark. Put on eight pounds –

LYDIA (*shouting*). Two!

MARK *castles.*

SEBASTIAN. The move of a coward.

After a pause.

How did we get to know each other, Mark? It was in California when I was lecturing at UCLA, but I don't remember exactly how – was it chess?

MARK. No, it was Lydia. I came to hear the new Tolstoy lecture and sat next to the new Tolstoy's wife.

SEBASTIAN. Oh yes, of course. You thought for a moment you were in love with her or something, didn't you?

MARK (*looking at* LYDIA). I think I still am – or something –

SEBASTIAN (*deep in the game*). Extraordinary.

LYDIA *picks up her wrap to have another go, but is warned by* MARK *with a gesture.*

How long ago was it that we had that fantastic scene?

MARK. Twenty-five years –

SEBASTIAN. Pissed as newts in a topless joint in downtown Los Angeles –

MARK. They didn't have topless joints then.

SEBASTIAN. Where was it?

MARK. Just a bar.

SEBASTIAN. It seemed rather topless, but I suppose everything did in those days. Did you ever tell Lydia about it?

LYDIA *has set herself firmly down again. The conversation
is interesting her.*

LYDIA. No, he didn't.

SEBASTIAN. Well he should have. It was all very funny,
really. (*To* MARK.) Knight to King's Bishop four, Mark.

MARK (*savagely*). I can see –

SEBASTIAN. Well you couldn't see anything that night.
I suppose I couldn't either, come to that.

(*To* LYDIA.) It was about four in the morning and Mark
suddenly threw his arms around me, shattering all the
glasses at the bar –

MARK. We were at a table, in a corner – and I shattered no
glasses.

SEBASTIAN (*sternly*). We were at the bar, you broke at least
six of their best pony glasses, and you startled an elderly
hooker almost to death –

MARK. A *topless* elderly hooker, of course. Don't listen to
him, Lydia, his memory's going rapidly . . . It's very sad –

SEBASTIAN (*to* LYDIA). You get the picture, darling. Mark
has thrown his arms around me and the cutlery has gone
flying –

LYDIA. Get to the dialogue.

SEBASTIAN. The dialogue . . . Yes. Well, suiting words to
his astonishing action, he said: 'Oh, what a pity it is that
I admire you so much more than any writer on earth, and
that I love you so very, very passionately . . . '

MARK. I never said 'passionately' –

SEBASTIAN. Well whatever the word was, it put that hooker
out like a light –

MARK. There was no hooker. He's inventing all this, Lydia . . .

LYDIA (*rapt*). Go on.

SEBASTIAN. So, naturally, I said: 'Why do you feel it a pity?' and he said:

Imitating a lachrymose drunk.

'Because, whatever I may feel for you, I feel far more for your wife, whom I want to – '

MARK. One thing's certain. I never said *'whom'*.

SEBASTIAN. My mistake. You wouldn't have. '*Who* I want to take away from you and live with for the rest of my life. And, what is more, who I intend to get to do just that with . . . ' The syntax went a bit at the end . . .

He waits for an appropriately laughing response from LYDIA. But she is merely sitting, chin on hand, staring.

LYDIA (*at length*). Go on.

SEBASTIAN. Well, so I said: 'Are you trying to tell me that you are in love with Lydia?'

Pause.

LYDIA. Can I give you the right inflection? 'Are you trying to tell me that you are in love with *Lydia*?'

Her inflections, undoubtedly the truthful ones, indicate profound amazement, some jocularity, and a vague certainty that MARK, in his tipsy state, must certainly have confused her with another woman, probably called 'Mavis'.

MARK. Good – I've moved, Sebastian. My Knight to Queen's Bishop three –

LYDIA. Let him go on with the story. What happened then?

SEBASTIAN. Well, I thought – here we are in this bar, and it's four o'clock, and we don't really want a brawl do we? Besides I couldn't very well hit an older man, with heart problems, too. So I decided on a course of correct English courtesy. I said: 'And what pray, leads you so suppose that

my wife, a lady of some taste and discernment, would care
to spend the rest of *her* life with some hairy old baboon
who couldn't write BUM on a wall and who, if he could,
would certainly spell it UMB?'

LYDIA. The *delicate* approach –

SEBASTIAN. I thought it best to take it lightly. I then settled
the bill, paid for the broken Waterford, took him to his dreadful English Tudor mansion in Beverly Hills, undressed him
lovingly, and put him to bed. In return for which I received
a passionate embrace –

MARK. *Not passionate!* I was never *passionate* –

SEBASTIAN. You were in no condition to judge . . .

Back to the board.

Knight to Queen's Bishop three? Interesting –

LYDIA. Is that the end of the story?

SEBASTIAN (*his back to her*). Oh yes, of course. How would
you have wanted it to end?

Pause.

LYDIA. The way it did, of course.

*She finishes her drink, and stares at the two heads, both
bent over the chess board.*

How else?

Pause

SEBASTIAN. Darling, don't you think it's time you started
our dinner?

LYDIA. Yes.

She goes up a couple of stairs.

Something tells me it's going tonight to taste a little pecul–
peculiarlar.

She goes into the kitchen. There is a very long pause.
SEBASTIAN *leans back abstractedly, murmuring.*

SEBASTIAN.

> Ay, but to die and go we know not where;
> To lie in cold obstruction and to rot;

MARK who has been about to make a move stops with his hand on the piece, staring at SEBASTIAN.

> This sensible warm motion to become
> A kneaded clod; and the delighted spirit –

Are you making that move?

MARK. I don't know yet. Is that Shakespeare?

SEBASTIAN.

> To be imprisoned in the viewless winds,
> And blown with restless violence round about
> The pendant world!

Can't keep your hand on it for ever, you know – as the Bishop said to the actress –

MARK. O.K. That's my move.

SEBASTIAN. And a bloody silly one too, if I might say so.

He considers, and then continues softly.

> The weariest and most loathed worldly life
> That age, ache, penury and imprisonment
> Can lay on nature, is a paradise
> To what we fear of death.

Yes, Shakespeare. One is forced to admit that he could sometimes sort out the words. Pessimistic old sod!

MARK. I thought he was a complacent old bourgeois.

SEBASTIAN. He was both – that's the trouble.

He moves.

This move will lead to your ultimate annihilation.

MARK. The Cruttwell variation? It has interest, if only fleeting.

He considers the board.

What made you choose that particular quotation?

SEBASTIAN. Hm? – Oh, it's in my article. The same man that wrote those lines also wrote:

We are such stuff as dreams are made on,
And our little life is rounded with a sleep.

Angrily.

Rounded with a sleep! Phooey! It's what we all hope, but do we know? See what I mean about the two Shakespeares? That last one's cosy, middle-class, comforting and commercial. But:

To be imprison'd in the viewless winds,
And blown with restless violence round about
The pendant world . . .

Can any of your modern, hippy poets top that? – Fellow wasn't consistent, you see.

MARK (*making a move*). Check.

A key turns in the front door and JOEY *comes in. His hair is long, but neat: his sweater and slacks are of sober hue. He looks what he is, a Liberal. He carries an overnight bag.*

SEBASTIAN (*not seeing him*). I think you have fallen right into my trap.

JOEY. Hullo, Dad.

Pause. Neither smiles.

SEBASTIAN. Are we expecting you?

JOEY. No.

With warmth.

Hullo, Mr Walters.

MARK (*getting up and shaking hands*). Hullo, Joey. You look ten years older than when I last saw you.

JOEY. I feel ten years older. You don't know what canvassing in a bye-election can do to one.

He puts down his bag. SEBASTIAN *contents himself with an abstracted Pah!*

MARK. Congratulations on getting a play done on TV, Joey. That's great.

JOEY. I'm scared to death. Anyway, seven-thirty. No one'll see it. No hope of you seeing it, is there?

MARK. Sure. I'm coming here tomorrow just for that.

JOEY (*awed*). Specially to see my play?

MARK. Yep.

JOEY. Jesus –

MARK. I'm sure it'll be great –

SEBASTIAN (*loudly*). Do you mind not yakkety-yakketing with my vote-splitting son? You are playing chess with me.

JOEY. Who's winning?

SEBASTIAN. I have him in a trap. It's only a question of how best to snap together its steel jaws.

JOEY *examines the game.*

JOEY. Looks the other way round to me.

SEBASTIAN (*snarling*). Do you mind?

JOEY. Sorry.

SEBASTIAN *puts his hand on a piece.* JOEY *hisses gently.* SEBASTIAN *withdraws it. Then he put his hand on another piece.* JOEY *hisses again.*

SEBASTIAN. Will you kindly cease your imitation of a cobra on heat? Faulty though it may seem to outside observers, I prefer my game to *be* my own.

JOEY. I just didn't want to see you lose your Knight.

SEBASTIAN (*who plainly hasn't seen*). My Knight?

JOEY. Two moves ahead –

SEBASTIAN (*after a pause*). Now a Knight sacrifice might well be my plan. How do you know it isn't, eh?

Nevertheless he withdraws his hand. After a moment he makes another move without hesitation.

JOEY. That's torn it.

SEBASTIAN (*explosively*). If you're so bloody good, why don't you ever play?

JOEY. I do.

SEBASTIAN. I meant with me.

Pause.

JOEY. Two reasons, I suppose. One, you don't ask me. Two, if I did win you'd call me a fascist pig.

SEBASTIAN. Meaning I'm a bad loser?

JOEY. Meaning that anyone who stamps on your ego is always a fascist pig.

SEBASTIAN. Go away, or I'll stamp on something more painful than your ego.

JOEY. I want to watch. You don't mind, do you Mr Walters?

MARK. Not at all.

SEBASTIAN (*calling*). Lydia! Lydia!

She comes out of the kitchen.

The brood is here. Remove it before I do it violence.

LYDIA (*with a joyous cry*). Joey!

She begins to run down the stairs. Thinks better of it and waits half-way down for him to bound up to her. There they have a warm embrace.

Joey! Oh, how marvellous!

She embraces him again.

SEBASTIAN (*to* MARK). Forgive her, Mark. She hasn't seen him for five days –

LYDIA. Why didn't you let us know? Have you eaten?

JOEY. Yes. I only knew myself at the lunch break. They don't need me until Election Day –

LYDIA. Thursday? And I've got you till then?

JOEY *nods.* SEBASTIAN *looks up at them.*

SEBASTIAN. I've got him too.

JOEY. Don't bother, Dad. I won't be in *your* way.

SEBASTIAN. Not till Election Day? Ha! That must mean your man's given up.

JOEY. He's got it made, Dad. The latest poll gives him twelve per cent over all other candidates.

SEBASTIAN. I don't believe it.

Rising to get a drink.

The electorate, God knows, can be utterly idiotic, but it's not raving mad.

LYDIA (*to* JOEY). Could you get your mother a little sip of vodka, dear?

JOEY. I didn't know you drank vodka.

LYDIA. I've rather taken to it in the last hour.

She sits carefully on the steps.

JOEY *comes down into the room to get her her drink.*

SEBASTIAN. How can a strong left-wing constituency suddenly go Liberal? It doesn't make sense.

JOEY. It makes perfect political sense for today. The electorate's got bored with the Right and the Left, so they're voting centre.

SEBASTIAN. Don't talk to me as if I were a cretinous ape who only involved himself in politics yesterday –

JOEY. No. It was quite a long time ago, wasn't it, Dad? When Hitler was the devil. Stalin was in his heaven and all was right with the world. Times have changed you know. You old-time Marxists are out of touch.

He takes the vodka up the stairs to his mother.

She strokes his hair.

SEBASTIAN. Out of touch, are we?

LYDIA (*to* JOEY). Careful dear.

> *To* SEBASTIAN.

> Did you ever have hair as beautiful as this?

SEBASTIAN. Much more beautiful. But I was in an army, fighting Fascism, and I was made to cut it short. That was for hygiene. Lice.

JOEY. Did you get many lice as an Intelligence Officer in Whitehall?

> *He has sat two steps down from his mother who seems bent on stroking his hair and whom he is never averse from having do so.*

SEBASTIAN. I was speaking figuratively.

JOEY. Figurative lice?

LYDIA (*hastily*). Don't annoy him. You know what'll happen.

JOEY (*ignoring her advice*). Do you know how many votes your Jim Grant's going to get?

SEBASTIAN. Who's my Jim Grant?

JOEY. You involve yourself in politics but you don't know the name of the candidates in the most important bye-election of the year?

SEBASTIAN. Well, if there was a Communist candidate –

JOEY (*returning to his mother*). There is. Jim Grant.

LYDIA (w*hispering in his ear*). Careful, dear.

SEBASTIAN. Well? How many votes is he going to get?

JOEY. Four hundred, if he's lucky.

SEBASTIAN. That's just a damn lie! In a working-class constituency like East Worsley –

JOEY. It isn't any more, Dad – at least the voters aren't bound in a fraternal brotherhood of cloth caps to vote against cigar-chewing bosses in top hats.

SEBASTIAN (*returning to his seat*). I don't wish to hear any more.

With dignity.

Wait till Thursday, my boy – that's all. Just wait till Thursday.

To MARK, *with sudden rage.*

Are you going to take all night?

MARK (*startled*). Sorry.

He makes his move.

JOEY. Mind you, Jim Grant's one of the nicest men and most brilliant speakers you're ever likely to meet. Very popular with everyone too. But – he's like you, Dad. He's out of touch. It's all talk. He really doesn't want action any more. We Liberals do.

SEBASTIAN. Flashing mirrors in the eyes of South African cricketers?

JOEY. We didn't do that. But we did get the tour stopped. And what did you do, Dad? Booked tickets for the London matches.

SEBASTIAN (*furiously*). And a fortune they cost me. Fifty quid down the drain because of you and your long-haired layabouts . . . (*Recovering himself.*) We mustn't flout the issue. A Centre Party is nothing more nor less than gross collaboration with the enemy.

LYDIA (*happily sipping*). Collaboration. That's very bad. We used to get shot for that – by both sides.

JOEY (*patting her hand*). Mum, that was a long time ago.

LYDIA. Yes, it was. It sometimes doesn't seem so.

JOEY (*to* SEBASTIAN). I suppose by 'the enemy' you mean the status quo.

SEBASTIAN (*looking at board*). What?

To JOEY.

I mean the whole, rotten stinking mess that is Britain as it is today.

JOEY. What, mum?

LYDIA *is whispering in* JOEY*'s ear.*

SEBASTIAN. What's she saying?

JOEY. She says 'Isn't it terrible, but she rather likes Britain as it is today.'

SEBASTIAN. She's pissed.

JOEY (*laughing*). Are you, Mum?

LYDIA. Well, it's not a very nice way of –

Firmly.

Yes, I am.

JOEY. Good for you.

MARK. What about America today? Do you know what the drop-out rate is among young people there now?

LYDIA. What's a drop-out?

MARK. A boy or girl who feels he just can't take our present civilisation and just – well – drops out.

LYDIA. Not – pushed or anything? Just – drops out?

MARK. Sure they're pushed. They're pushed by the squalor and degradation of life in America today.

LYDIA (*to herself, happily*). Squalor-and-degradation –

JOEY (*getting up from the steps*). Dad, I'm not denying that all of us today, on both sides of the Atlantic, are living in a nightmare. But we want to *do* something –

LYDIA (*to herself*). Nightmare –

She titters, still happy.

SEBASTIAN. Darling, are you going to sit there just repeating everything we say?

LYDIA (*defiantly*). Yes, if I want to.

SEBASTIAN. You don't think a touch of light cooking might be in order?

LYDIA. I like this discussion.

SEBASTIAN. Well you're not making a great contribution to it.

LYDIA. How can I make a contrib – join in your discussion? I don't belong to this country.

JOEY. Mum, you do.

LYDIA. No. I'm an Englishwoman – thanks only to the lucky accident of a British Intelligence Officer having a night-out in the Russian Zone of Berlin, and stopping off at Bentinck Strasse sixteen.

SEBASTIAN. For God's sake, Lydia, Joey mightn't know we met in a – in an establishment.

LYDIA. A 'Maison de Rendezvous' is what I've always called it.

JOEY (*to* SEBASTIAN). Don't worry, Dad, I knew where you met Mum.

SEBASTIAN. Good. But it's not a thing to go roaring from all the roof tops in Islington.

LYDIA. I was not roaring it from all the roof tops in Islington. I was simply saying that I belong to where I was born, the Republic of Estonia. A rather small country – about twice the size of Wales, with a slightly better climate than Finland, our neighbour to the North.

She rises with a little help from the banisters.

Now I'm afraid I can't tell you gentlemen just how night-marish Estonia is today, because, you see, there isn't an Estonia. Estonia has ceased to exist. So I have no country at all. None at all. Which I'm quite sure is making all you English and Americans cry like billy-oh.

SEBASTIAN. Darling, you must be careful of your idioms. 'Billy-oh' is very old-fashioned –

LYDIA. Yes, it must be. I learnt it in school in Tallinn. That's our capital city – was our capital city. So all I'm entitled to say about Britain today is that it has been a rather pleasant place for an Estonian to have lived in. I shall now go and cook.

SEBASTIAN. Yes, darling. Good idea.

To MARK, *sotto voce.*

Forgive the refugee bit. She doesn't do it much.

JOEY (*smiling*). To *have* lived in, Mum? Why? Are you planning to leave?

LYDIA *suddenly clutches* JOEY *in a fierce embrace. He is surprised.* LYDIA *recovers quickly.*

LYDIA (*in a 'matter of fact' voice*). I meant up to now, Joey, of course.

She turns, takes a step or two quite firmly away from him, then sways – not drunkenly – and holds on tight to the banisters, her body suddenly rigid.

Do you know – I think – perhaps –

JOEY, *puzzled goes towards her.* SEBASTIAN *moves with extraordinary quickness to reach her before* JOEY, *whom he roughly pushes back so that he nearly falls.*

To SEBASTIAN.

Bed?

SEBASTIAN. Yes, darling. A very good idea.

He has his arm firmly supporting her.

Now just one step in front of the other.

She manages a couple of steps.

That's very clever. It's called walking.

LYDIA. Dinner – can Joey – ?

SEBASTIAN. Yes, of course he can. Now another two steps.

She manages them.

That's it. We're doing fine. You can manage dinner, can't you, Joey?

JOEY. Yes, dad.

LYDIA. I'm pissed, that's all.

SEBASTIAN. Yes, darling. That's exactly what I'd say you are.

And as a newt.

To the others.

It's quite a shock, after all these years, to find one has a wife with a drink problem – instead of being just a drunk, like me.

LYDIA. I love you.

To JOEY.

And I love you.

To MARK.

And you. I love you all –

SEBASTIAN. Yes, darling, that's very nice for us all to know, I'm sure.

LYDIA. And I love England –

Seeing MARK.

– and America –

She stares again at JOEY.

Left, Right and – Centre –

SEBASTIAN. Yes, I'm sure that all parties in England and America will be delighted to hear that. We'll issue a communiqué later. Now if you could just manoeuvre your arse round this bend – that's it.

To MARK.

My move would have been Pawn to Queen's Rook three – Now, darling, two tiny little steps – well done. Now a little more of this one foot after the other lark. Who knows? You might even get to like it –

The lights fade.

Act Two

The lights come on to show the same room. It is the following night, and the television has been pulled out of its corner to a position where it can be clearly seen from any one of four chairs which JOEY *is in the process of carefully arranging. He is dressed as the evening before, except perhaps for a differently coloured sweater. Finished with his meticulous arrangement of the chairs, he inspects the various dishes evidently prepared by* LYDIA *for the night's occasion.*

JOEY (*calling*). Mum!

LYDIA (*from the kitchen*). Yes, darling?

JOEY. What will they all be drinking?

LYDIA (*from the kitchen*). Leave that to me.

JOEY. O.K.

> *He kneels down and turns on the television. A* VOICE *comes on loudly, fades and then comes on again.*

VOICE. Well, I can only repeat what I've just said. It's the Government's responsibility to govern – that's true, none of us have ever denied it – but a bad law is still a bad law whatever government has passed it –

> JOEY *turns the volume control down to silent, and manipulates the other controls.* JOEY'*s tense face is illuminated by the picture that he sees and we don't.*

> LYDIA *appears from the kitchen with a tray on which is a bottle of champagne and three glasses.*

LYDIA. This is what they'll be drinking.

JOEY. Oh Mum. That's making too much of it.

LYDIA. You can't make too much of it.

She has honoured the occasion with a becoming long dress.
JOEY *takes the tray from her.*

Nervous?

JOEY. Petrified. Why only three glasses?

LYDIA. Darling, if you forgive me, I think I'll stick to Vichy water.

She sits down, exhausted.

That ought to go in a bucket. There's one in the kitchen. Put quite a lot of ice in it. It's been in the fridge but it'll look better.

JOEY. Are you feeling better?

LYDIA. Yes. But how dare the Americans try and make vodka? Go and get that ice.

JOEY. And another glass –

LYDIA. All right. Just a sip, in your honour.

JOEY (*looking at his watch*). You don't suppose Dad's forgotten, do you?

LYDIA. Of course not. He's been talking of nothing else all day. Go on.

JOEY. Where is he?

LYDIA. They wanted him at the office. An obituary or something. He'll be well on his way back by now.

JOEY. Did you call him?

LYDIA. Yes. He said he'd be back in plenty of time.

JOEY. Good.

He runs up the stairs.

LYDIA. And Joey –

She makes the correct sign.

Merde.

JOEY (*smiling*). Thanks.

He goes into kitchen.

The second he has gone LYDIA *is on her feet, walking quickly and silently towards the telephone. She looks up a number in a private book, then dials with speed.*

LYDIA (*into receiver*). Mrs Larkin? – Lydia Cruttwell. I'm sorry to be embarrassing, but this is a crisis. Is Sebastian with you? – I see. Well, when did your little chat finish? Over an hour ago. Where was he going? – Please, Mrs Larkin, this isn't a jealous wife. I'm not jealous – I'm pleased, really. But this is important, dreadfully important – No clue at all? During your chat did he happen to mention that his son had a television play on this evening? – Yes. BBC2, 7.30 – Thank you – Yes. Only twenty – thank you. Yes, that's the crisis – Something worse? What *could* be worse? – Well, he sometimes goes to his Editor's flat after your chats. Did he say anything? – Meet some friends? Where? – Well, what's his favourite haunt up your way? After your flat, of course –

Her face grows despairing.

But I can't ring all those. Please try and help. I've got to find out where he –

She stops abruptly as JOEY *appears with the bucket and an extra glass. Laughing gaily.*

Oh, that's terribly sweet of you, darling – angelic of you to ask us, but I know Sebastian can't. He gets so tied up in the evenings – it's when he works you know –

She smiles happily at JOEY.

I'll get him to call you. He's due in any second. Goodbye.

To JOEY.

What a bore that woman is!

JOEY. Who?

LYDIA. No-one you know. An old woman called Rhoda Robinson. Always trying to get us out for cocktails –

JOEY. I didn't hear the telephone ring –

LYDIA. That happens to me when *I'm* getting ice.

The doorbell rings. Distractedly.

That's Mark. Answer it darling.

JOEY runs to the door. MARK is outside. He has graced the evening with a dinner jacket.

MARK (*shaking hands*). Well, Joey, here's wishing you every-thing.

JOEY. Gosh, Mr Walters, you didn't change for me?

MARK. Of course. Always dress for a premiere. Here's a little sprig of heather for luck –

The sprig of heather is fairly easily recognisable as a small Cartier box. MARK comes into the room and kisses LYDIA.

Evening, Lydia.

LYDIA (*gratefully*). Marcus.

They kiss. JOEY meanwhile is opening his present. They are cuff-links.

JOEY. Are these cuff-links?

LYDIA (*looking at them*). No, they're ear-rings, and they're meant for me.

To MARK.

What are you trying to do, Mark? Keep the whole Cruttwell family?

MARK. Well, this is a very important occasion – the début of a brilliant young dramatist.

JOEY. Dramatist – gosh – you don't get called dramatist till you're dead.

LYDIA. He let 'brilliant' pass.

JOEY. No I didn't, Mum. I just closed my ears.

Engrossed in his cuff-links.

I don't think I've ever had a present like this.

Belatedly.

Of course Mum's given me some smashing things –

LYDIA (*arm around him*). Smashing. Nickel cigarette lighters, plastic Indian beads. Joey's going to look after Sebastian while we're away –

MARK. Where's Sebastian?

Pointing to the work-room.

Is he in there?

LYDIA (*calmly*). No.

Looking at her watch.

He's been at the office, but he's due back any minute.

To JOEY.

Don't you think you should wear those cuff-links – for luck?

JOEY. I haven't got a shirt – I mean for links.

LYDIA. Borrow one of your father's.

JOEY (*slightly dismayed*). Does that mean a tie?

LYDIA. Oh no. Don't betray your convictions.

JOEY *bounds up the stairs and off.* LYDIA *instantly becomes tense.*

Mark, Sebastian's lost. It's a hundred to one he's forgotten –

MARK. Oh God, no –

LYDIA. Go down, do you mind? There's a call-box at the end of the street. Have you got change?

MARK (*feeling*). How much now?

LYDIA. Two p.

MARK. Jesus, this inflation. O.K.

LYDIA. Call this number here. Remember it?

MARK. Of course.

LYDIA. I'll answer.

She is hustling him towards the door.

I'll tell Joey you're reparking your car, or something –

MARK. What shall I say?

LYDIA. You don't need to say anything. I'll do the talking. Wait a moment.

She runs to the desk, takes out an envelope and scribbles on it. Then she gives it to him.

Is that clear. My hand is so shaking with rage –

MARK (*reading*). 'Sebastian – If after 7.30 go away until well after eight. And then, the first thing you say is "Congratulations, Joey." I'm covering for you.'

LYDIA. Not even *he* can fail to follow that, can he?

She opens the door, licks the flap of the envelope, and sticks it to the door.

MARK. He can do some funny things.

LYDIA. You see how I'm laughing in anticipation.

JOEY comes running down the stairs, wearing a shirt much too large for him, outside his slacks.

For Joe's sake. Tell the policeman you're a foreigner, Mark. That always works – wait – here's the latch-key –

She gives him a key and then closes the door quickly in his face.

To JOEY.

Americans always park their cars in the middle of the street.

JOEY. He won't miss anything?

He looks at his watch. LYDIA *coming calmly towards him slaps his hand.*

LYDIA. Plenty of time, dear. Don't fuss. You want me to fix these for you?

JOEY. Yes, please. They're complicated.

LYDIA *attends to fixing the links.*

Your hands are shaking, too.

LYDIA. Well, of course, I'm nervous –

Pause.

JOEY. Are you sure Dad hasn't forgotten?

LYDIA. Positive.

JOEY. I hope he's not late. If you miss the beginning it's difficult to follow.

LYDIA. His opinion means a lot to you doesn't it?

JOEY. Well – after all – one of the best critics in the world –

LYDIA. Not *the* best?

JOEY. How do I know? I don't read them all.

Regarding his links.

But I'd say that on his day he's about the best I've read.

LYDIA. You *admire* him, then, Joey?

JOEY (*impatiently*). I just said so.

Referring to his links.

Gosh, aren't these something?

LYDIA (*admiring them*). Something is certainly what they are, Joey. After what you've just said about Sebastian, now might be the moment to ask you to do me a little favour –

JOEY (*guardedly*). Mum I only said I liked him as a *critic*. I didn't say –

LYDIA. I said: 'Do *me* a favour,' Joey.

JOEY (*very defensive*). Something to do with Dad?

LYDIA. Yes.

JOEY. What?

Pause.

LYDIA. You took over very well last night, I hear, after your mother got herself a little – over-excited. You cooked a very good dinner . . .

JOEY. I only finished off what you'd got ready.

LYDIA. Your father said it was very good. And after that, he said, you washed up brilliantly.

JOEY. How can you wash up brilliantly? I mean either you wash up or you don't, and as my seniors were plainly bent on shouting insults at each other over the chess-board until about five in the morning, I thought if I'm going to get to bed at all I'd better wash up, now and alone. That's all, Mum. It's not worth three columns in next week's *Sunday Times* –

LYDIA. Still you did it.

JOEY (*in deepest suspicion*). Yes, I did. So?

Pause.

LYDIA. Now I told you, didn't I, that I was going off on a little holiday next week?

JOEY (*even more suspiciously*). Yes, Mum.

LYDIA. And that means that for about ten days your father's going to be all on his own.

After no response from JOEY.

All on his ownsome, Joey –

JOEY (*interrupting shrilly*). No, Mum. No! No! Not in a thousand years –

LYDIA. But Joey, your father would be so pleased –

JOEY. He'd be round the bend in twenty-four hours, and so would I.

LYDIA. That's not true. Now, let's think, you haven't got anything on for the next ten days, have you?

JOEY. I will have now.

LYDIA. You have to pay Jerry and Sue a pound a night for that room don't you?

JOEY. I'll pay them ten pounds a night for the next ten days. It'd be cheap at the price.

Pause.

LYDIA (*laughing politely*). You know, Joey, if you stayed on here for that – very short time – your father would be so awfully – touched – Really – I mean *touched,* Joey.

She knows it's a phony word as soon as she uttered it.

JOEY (*shrill again*). *Touched?* Are you bonkers? *Touched?* *Father?* He wouldn't be touched if I jumped in front of a bus to save him from getting hit by it. He'd just come back and say:

Imitating him better than does LYDIA.

'Extraordinary thing just happened, darling. A bus nearly hit me. I think I'll sue London Transport.' And you'd say: 'Where's Joey?' And he'd say: 'Joey? Now, why isn't he here – Oh yes, I remember . . . He's lying under a bus, somewhere.' –

LYDIA (*after trying to be angry, has to laugh*). You seem to have inherited your father's creative talent.

JOEY (*looking at his watch*). Well, that's yet to be proved, isn't it, in about seventeen minutes.

In alarm.

Mum, do you think he's going to make it?

LYDIA (*bravely*). Of course, he's going to make it. You know, Joey – I think, somehow, you mean rather a lot to him –

JOEY. Oh Mum, no one means a lot to him, and you know it. Not even you.

LYDIA. Now that's a very bad thing to say.

JOEY. Yes it is, but it's the truth. And one has to tell the truth.

LYDIA. Has one?

JOEY. Honesty, in this life, is just about the only thing that matters.

LYDIA. Is it?

JOEY. We both know that the only person who matters to Dad is Dad. Mum, you've admitted that to me often enough –

LYDIA. As a joke, perhaps.

JOEY. No, Mum, as the truth. Don't be dishonest, Mum, please . . .

Eagerly.

Is that him?

He listens intently. LYDIA *pretends to.*

LYDIA. No. It's Mr Jackson upstairs. But he'll come. Don't worry.

JOEY. Oh, I don't worry. If he wants to miss it, let him miss it!

LYDIA. He won't . . . Darling, I think you do mean something rather special to him –

JOEY. A rather special punch-bag –

LYDIA (*hotly*). That's not true. You hit him far more often than he hits you.

JOEY. Yes. Because he still sees me as a tiny little Joeykins, who has to have the great Marxist truth spanked into his little tummy every now and then. He doesn't realise I'm grown up, and I've got my own truth now, which I've learnt myself and I can sometimes get in a couple of quick left hooks into *his* little tummy before he's squared up –

LYDIA. A bit below the belt, sometimes, aren't they?

JOEY. Well that's where he *should* expect them, as he still sees me *that* high . . .

He indicates some object about two feet high.

Mum, his political thinking isn't just out of date – God, did Stalin prove *nothing?* – it's so *dishonest*!

LYDIA (*glancing at the telephone, absently*). Which, in your view, is the greatest crime of all?

JOEY. Yes, it is. Dad only spouts red revolution as a kind of spell to prevent it ever happening. The way some old people talk about death – you know the kind – ?

LYDIA. Yes. I sympathise a bit –

JOEY. I think it's utterly squalid and corrupt to spout a theory when you personally would hate it coming true. Imagine Dad being ordered by his State-controlled Sunday paper to say that Evelyn Waugh was a bad writer: or that Orwell was a lackey of the Bourgeoisie? He'd be in a Labour Camp in a week.

LYDIA. These days I believe it's a Mental Home –

JOEY. I'm sorry. I was forgetting about your family.

LYDIA. Don't be. It was a very long time ago. Anyway, at least you grant him some integrity –

JOEY. About literature, yes . . . The highest. But about politics, no . . . The lowest. Ten days of the two of us together alone would be disaster, Mum. Please believe it. Either there'd be parricide or the opposite – what's it called – ?

LYDIA (*looking at the telephone*). What's *what* called?

JOEY. The killing of a son by a father?

LYDIA (*automatically*). I don't know. You must ask your father.

JOEY (*equally automatically*). Yes, I will. It's 'felicide', I suppose.

LYDIA. I suppose so . . . So you won't do this for *me*, Joey? For *me*, I asked?

JOEY. Mum, I'll do anything for you. You know that. Anything in the world. But not that. Forgive me.

Pause.

LYDIA. You see he did like so much what you did for him last night –

JOEY (*laughing*). Oh, Mum!

Pause.

LYDIA (*serious*). And I do kind of hate him being left quite alone –

Pause.

JOEY. Do you have to go?

LYDIA. Yes, I do. I can't get out of it – And then I may have to go away again, perhaps even for a bit longer –

JOEY. When?

LYDIA. Oh, not yet. Not soon. But there was this talk about my, perhaps, starting up something of my own sometime –

JOEY. Doing what?

LYDIA. Oh – like going back to Estonia, writing some articles about it – even a book. Joey, your father's so *helpless* alone –

JOEY. Well, whose fault is that?

LYDIA. 'Whose fault' is only an argument, never a reason.

Pause.

JOEY. Mum. It will be disastrous, he hasn't changed, he's really a very high old Tory. When there was that revolt in Czechoslovakia and the Russians went in to squash it, I was only fifteen, but I remember listening to Dad and even then I was thinking but that's any old member of the Carlton Club saying: 'By God, sir, send in a few tanks – that'll teach the natives to know their place.' And I bet at the time of Hungary he was shouting; 'Send a gunboat up the Danube.' Wasn't he?

LYDIA is trying loyally not to laugh but has to give way before she can answer.

LYDIA. Very likely.

JOEY. Sorry, Mum. Now I'm grown up I'm answering back, and he hates it. It just won't work. I know it won't.

LYDIA. Are politics all that important? Joey, if there's one thing I've learnt from a fairly – hectic – life, it's that things – beliefs, creeds, ideas, theories – are so far, far less important than people. Honestly, Joey – in the end you'll find it's only people who matter at all.

Pause.

JOEY. I don't agree, but say you're right. He's a person, so am I. We're people. But we're on different wave lengths – Look,

I'll give you this. He has tried to communicate with me.
Sometimes, in what he thinks is my language, with words
like 'cool' and 'hep' and 'with it' and – oh everything.
I know he expects me to answer him in a hippy drawl like,
man, like it's real groovy man, like it blew my mind, man –

Hands over face.

Oh, Mum, it's so embarrassing! That's the way the over-
thirties talk – and he's over fifty.

LYDIA (*sharply*). Only just. How do you under-thirties talk?

JOEY. Well, you've heard me, and Jacky and Sue. We try to talk
English – the way he did when he was young. I suppose – a
bit less Mandarin, I hope. But English.

LYDIA. If it's just a question of idiom –

JOEY. Mum. I'm sorry. I can't stay on. It just isn't possible.

LYDIA. Joey, sons have always turned against their fathers all
through history. Sebastian turned against his –

JOEY. The Bishop?

He laughs.

Yes, I feel sorry for the Bishop –

He bends down to put the television on.

Just warming it up.

The telephone rings. LYDIA *crosses to it, muttering to
herself.*

LYDIA. Oh, thank God.

To JOEY.

Believe me, Joey, he does love you really, he does.

Into receiver.

Oh hullo! Hullo, darling! We were getting worried. Where
are you? – You're going to watch it there – with the Editor?
You mean he's going to watch too?

JOEY. Gosh! Is it colour?

LYDIA. Is it colour, Joey wants to know? – Very latest, of
course . . .

JOEY. Will the others be watching it too?

LYDIA (*into receiver*). Will the others be watching it too?

To JOEY.

All the others. Some very important people too.

JOEY. Gosh! – Oh gosh! Oh Jesus!

LYDIA. Hurry back, darling. You mustn't miss the beginning.
I gather if you do you'll find it rather hard to understand the
rest . . . Yes, darling. But hurry!

She rings off.

You see, Joey – you see!

JOEY. Surprise, surprise!

LYDIA. I hope now you're ashamed of yourself, You see how
much he cares?

JOEY. I bet it was your idea. To get his Editor to watch. I bet
that was your idea –

LYDIA. No, it was entirely his own idea.

JOEY. Ha, ha.

LYDIA. Are you implying I'm a liar?

JOEY. Well – I bet you used pressure.

LYDIA. Now, Joey, what pressure have I ever been able to
bring on your father to do something he didn't want to do?

JOEY. There you are. You're admitting it.

LYDIA. What?

JOEY. That he's a selfish old beast who thinks only of his own
comfort.

LYDIA (*sharply*). Joey, I won't have you talking about your
father like that – do you understand!

JOEY. Yes, Mum.

LYDIA. Especially after this – very – generous thing he's doing for you tonight. Going all that way up to Fleet Street?

JOEY (*embracing her*). Yes, I'm sorry.

LYDIA (*still trying to be angry*). And getting his Editor –

JOEY. Yes, I know, I know. I'm sorry.

Pause. LYDIA *looks down at his head, bravely resisting the almost overpowering instinct to stroke it.*

LYDIA. So shall we take it that you'll do what I've just asked?

No reply from JOEY. LYDIA *correctly takes it as a 'yes'.*

Good. Now I know that during those ten days you're going to find out a lot more about him –

JOEY (*his face on her shoulder*). Oh God, I hope not.

LYDIA. I mean what he's really like.

JOEY (*despondently*). I know what he's really like.

LYDIA. You don't, and I've just proved to you that you don't. Haven't I?

Pause. JOEY *releases himself from* LYDIA.

JOEY. There's some conspiracy on here. I don't know what it is, but I can feel it. I mean Dad *can't* want me to be alone with him for ten days –

LYDIA. Why not?

JOEY. Ten *whole* days? It's not possible.

LYDIA. Anything is possible in this life, Joey.

JOEY. Not that. Every time I open my mouth I enrage him.

LYDIA. Then don't open your mouth.

JOEY. I'll have to, sometimes.

LYDIA. Then think of opening it to say something pleasing –

JOEY (*suspiciously*). Like what?

LYDIA. Like saying that you think he's one of the best critics in the world –

Pause.

JOEY. I've tried that, and what always happened? I get my teeth kicked in.

LYDIA. Then slip those teeth in your pocket, talk through pursed lips and pretend you're not hurt.

JOEY. Which is what you've always done?

LYDIA *shrugs.*

But hell, Mum, that's *dishonest.*

LYDIA. Of course.

JOEY. And honesty –

LYDIA. Is just about the only thing in life that matters? I know, but you're wrong, Joey. Honesty between people who love each other, or let's say who should love each other, is the thing that matters least in this life.

JOEY (*outraged*). We should *pretend*, you mean?

LYDIA. Pretend like hell.

JOEY. You mean pretend that some half-assed political theory is a great truth?

LYDIA. Why not – provided *you* know it isn't.

JOEY. Pretend to agree with someone when you don't?

LYDIA. Why not – provided you *don't* agree with him.

JOEY. But – but that's just – politeness.

LYDIA. Anything wrong with that?

JOEY. Oh, a lot, these days. You see, Mum, it's –

LYDIA. Dishonest. Oh God, please let's have a little return to dishonesty! It was such a much happier world when people told us little lies about ourselves.

JOEY. You'll be talking of 'manners' next.

LYDIA. Yes, I will.

JOEY (*scornfully*). Mum, really! Manners Makyth Man!

LYDIA (*angrily*). Yes they do, and they makyth other men feel better. It's what I said earlier, Joey. It's people that count, not things – Look at Mark . . .

Muttering.

And where the hell *is* he? . . . Anyway look at Mark. When a writer of his standing takes the trouble to come out to Islington to see a half-hour first play by a twenty-year-old acquaintance, puts on a black tie, and says something pleasant about the début of a brilliant young dramatist – to say nothing about those bloody links – doesn't that make you feel well – good? Or is honesty so goddam important to you that you'd rather he'd taken one of his three London blonde tricks to the Talk of the Town and on to bed?

The door opens and MARK *comes in, panting.*

LYDIA (*brightly*). Oh hullo. We were just talking about you.

MARK (*falling into a chair*). Nicely, I hope.

LYDIA (*to* JOEY). Nicely, Joey?

JOEY (*turning away abruptly*). Mum was saying it. I was just listening –

MARK. But you were agreeing with her, I hope.

JOEY, *at the television set, and plainly disturbed, doesn't answer.*

LYDIA. Were you agreeing with me, Joey?

JOEY (*quietly*). Yes, Mum.

He fingers the dials.

LYDIA. Oh Mark, I've found my replacement.

MARK (*still panting, muttering*). Your replacement, your replacement, your –

Getting it.

Oh, your *replacement*?

LYDIA. Joey has very sweetly, and quite off his own bat, *volunteered* –

MARK. Well, isn't that swell?

As JOEY doesn't turn from the TV set, we must assume that he has done just that thing. The volume is down.

JOEY. Are those faces too green?

MARK. They look just right to me.

Pause.

LYDIA (*rather loudly*). Sebastian called while you were out, Mark.

MARK. Did he? Sebastian? Did he indeed?

LYDIA. Yes. He's going to see it on a much better set than this.

MARK (*almost too loud. LYDIA has to frown at him*). Oh really? Where?

JOEY (*turning, eagerly*). At his Editor's.

MARK (*back to normal*). Well, now, isn't that something!

LYDIA. You'd better sit here, Mark.

JOEY. No, Mum, I want you to sit there –

He indicates an armchair.

– and, Mr Walters, you there.

He indicates a rather uncomfortable-looking stool.

LYDIA. But this is more comfortable –

JOEY. I know. It's for you.

MARK. Ah, I get it. He wants his audience attentive.

LYDIA. Well, I'm his audience.

MARK (*sitting in the uncomfortable seat*). You're his mother.

JOEY (*from the set*). Sh!

He turns the set's volume up.

ANNOUNCER. On BBC1, in thirty seconds time, there is Match of the Week –

JOEY. Of course that's what they'll all be watching.

LYDIA. Nonsense.

ANNOUNCER. (*through this*). Meanwhile on BBC2 there follows shortly a new thirty-minute play in the current series: Youth Theatre, entitled 'The Trial of Maxwell Henry Peabody', by Joseph Cruttwell.

There is music.

LYDIA (*sharply*). *Joseph*! Why Joseph?

JOEY. It sounds more like a writer.

MARK. Yeah. It's a good name, Lydia. Joey's not too good. Joseph Cruttwell sounds like something –

JOEY. Thank you, Mr Walters.

The music stops.

FIRST VOICE (*loudly*). Maxwell Henry Peabody – come into court.

There is the sound of marching feet. LYDIA and MARK are both forward in that attitude of strained attention natural to people watching a TV play under the observant scrutiny of the author, who has chosen a vantage point where he can see both screen and audience.

The lights fade very quickly. There is a blackout for only a second before they come on again. LYDIA, MARK and JOEY are in exactly the same strained attitudes as before. One might think no one has moved even a finger to scratch his or her nose.

Have you anything to say why sentence should not be passed against you?

SECOND VOICE. But this is ridiculous. I have done nothing, I tell you – nothing, nothing, nothing –

FIRST VOICE. I agree. You have done nothing. Nothing to help your fellow human beings, nothing to save the world from the abyss into which it must soon finally fall, nothing save for your own material advantage –

SECOND VOICE. And my wife's. She's a director of several of my companies.

FIRST VOICE. And what did you do to save your son?

There is mocking laughter, followed by a blare of music, evidently signalling the end. Credits must follow because JOEY kneels by the set, his nose practically touching it, to see his name go by. LYDIA crouches with him.

LYDIA. There. Look how big his name is, Mark. Yes, Joseph is better.

She embraces him.

Darling, I'm so proud.

JOEY (*impatiently*). But did you *like* it?

LYDIA. I loved it, Joey

JOEY (*staring at her, puzzled*). Did it make you cry?

LYDIA. A little. Wasn't it meant to?

JOEY (*doubtfully*). Well it's really supposed to make one angry.

LYDIA (*reassuringly*). Oh it did that too.

MARK (*choosing his words*). Congratulations, young man, on a fine achievement –

The front door is unlocked. SEBASTIAN appears, looking angry, holding in his hand LYDIA's message which he has torn from the door.

SEBASTIAN. What in hell's this? If after seven-thirty don't come in. I'm covering up –

He stops at sight of the television set in its prominent position, of LYDIA in her smart dress, of MARK in a dinner jacket and of JOEY in one of his own shirts, all staring at him with varying expressions.

Oh Christ –

JOEY *looks away from him first.*

JOEY. Good night, Mum. Thanks for watching.

LYDIA. But the champagne –

JOEY. No, thanks. Good night, Mr Walters. Thanks for coming and for these.

He indicates the cuff-links.

And for what you said.

MARK. It was good – real good, Joey. I mean it.

JOEY. Thanks.

In silence he walks up the stairs, hoping evidently to achieve dignity. But coming to the end he hurries his steps in a revealing way. LYDIA *looks after him.*

SEBASTIAN. Oh Lord –

LYDIA *suddenly swings one fist at him, and then the other. They are hard blows, with real fury behind them, and both connect.* SEBASTIAN, *off balance, and slightly unsteady anyhow, is knocked off his feet and falls, upsetting a table.*

LYDIA (*with deep hatred*). You bastard!

She turns and runs up the stairs after her son. SEBASTIAN *stays where he is, for a moment, putting his hand to his cheek, and shaking his head.* MARK *helps him to his feet.*

SEBASTIAN (*indicating television*). Was it terrible?

MARK. Pretty terrible.

SEBASTIAN (*in a chair*). Get me a drink.

MARK. What is it? Scotch?

SEBASTIAN (*angrily*). Of course Scotch.

With a deep sigh.

Oh, my God! I had it written down, I'd tied knots in every-thing, I'd remembered it at lunch –

He takes the drink from MARK.

And then after lunch something happened –

Pause. He stares into his glass.

A perfect excuse, I suppose, if I could use it. Perfect. But I can't.

MARK. What was it?

SEBASTIAN. I can't tell you either. Except –

He stares into his glass again.

I have to anyway – but not as an excuse.

Loudly.

I have no excuses. I am as God made me, which is an uncaring shit. Oh damn! Poor little bugger. She'd covered up for me?

MARK. You were watching it with your Editor.

SEBASTIAN. He's in Tangier.

MARK. The kid wouldn't have known that.

SEBASTIAN. Damn silly cover. I suppose it might have worked though. She'd have made it work! – I'm not saying I didn't *deserve* a left hook, I'm just asking if you know why it was particularly savage?

MARK. Really want to know?

SEBASTIAN. Yes.

MARK. She'd just got him to promise to stay here with you those ten days she's away –

SEBASTIAN. Stay here with me? Why?

MARK. She thought – you might need company –

SEBASTIAN. His company? Why?

MARK. She just thought you might like it.

Pause. Quite a long one.

SEBASTIAN. But *he'd* hate it.

MARK. She'd got him to say yes.

Another pause.

SEBASTIAN (*covering his face*). Goddam it.

MARK. Yes.

SEBASTIAN. How has she been otherwise tonight, apart from first attempting to win the Nobel Peace Prize – and then turning into Muhammad Ali?

MARK. Oh, fine, I thought.

SEBASTIAN. Fine, you thought. Did you look at all?

MARK. Sure. She didn't look too well, but I don't suppose she is, after her pass-out last night. Hungover, I'd say.

SEBASTIAN. Yes. Well, you'd better brace yourself, I suppose. Have you got a drink?

Mark holds his up.

You're rather fond of this girl, aren't you?

MARK. I love her.

SEBASTIAN. And I suppose you're what might laughingly be called one of my best friends?

Finishing his drink.

Fill it up for me, would you?

MARK. Sure.

SEBASTIAN. Are you?

MARK. I think you are what you just said God made you, Sebastian – but maybe I'm not all that choosey about my best friends.

SEBASTIAN. Well I'm not either, or I wouldn't choose an ignorant, illiterate porn-monger –

MARK (*returning with the drink*). O.K. O.K. I'm braced.

SEBASTIAN. That wasn't a pass-out last night – not an ordinary one. It was a small stroke.

Pause.

MARK. How do you know?

SEBASTIAN. She's had them before, and these last months they're getting more frequent. It's one of the things I've been told to look out for, you see – and it's one of the things you've got to look out for too when you take her away. I've got a list somewhere –

MARK. Surely the vodka –

SEBASTIAN. It probably helped – that and the cortisone – so don't let her wallow in the stuff as I did last night. She's been off any drink at all for over six months – so go fairly easy out there. Mind you the odd piss-up won't make much difference. Here's that list. Now I've got the doctor's address in Monte Carlo somewhere too –

He fumbles in his pockets again.

MARK (*quietly*). Did you say cortisone?

SEBASTIAN. What? Yes. She's been on it six weeks. She doesn't know it, of course. Thinks they're iron pills, or something. Old Conny Schuster – he's her doctor – 'Uncle Constantin' she calls him – an ex-Estonian – he's quite a wonder. He can get her to believe anything – where the hell did I put that address? Ah, here it is. Docteur Villoret. Address is on it.

MARK takes it from him.

Conny Schuster called him this afternoon, so he'll be wise to the situation, as your horrible phrase goes.

MARK. Could you, perhaps, put me wise too?

Pause. SEBASTIAN looks up at him.

SEBASTIAN. I suppose so. I've been trying to put it off. I can't put it off any longer, can I?

Another pause.

She's in the terminal stages of a disease called poly-arteritis. You've probably never heard of it because it isn't very common. It comes from malnutrition early in life.

Pause. SEBASTIAN gets up and takes MARK's glass to fill, patting his arm as he goes.

Sorry, I had to tell you, you see, because old Conny
Schuster wouldn't have let her go otherwise, unless I was
along. I'm well-briefed, you see. What's that dreadful drink
you have?

MARK. Bourbon. Did you say terminal?

SEBASTIAN. Yes.

MARK. How long does that mean?

SEBASTIAN. Three or four months. Six at most.

He hands MARK *the drink.*

MARK. Are you positive?

SEBASTIAN *laughs.*

SEBASTIAN. That's just the word, I'm afraid.

He pulls another paper from his pocket and hands it to
MARK.

This came from Conny Schuster by hand to the office this
afternoon. He'd had it early this morning from the hospital,
but couldn't call me because of Lydia. You see there: 'Poly-
arteritis'. 'Acute' – Positive.

MARK *stares at the paper with unseeing eyes. He knows,
after all, its contents. Then he hands it back. Pause.*

MARK (*at length*). So that's the something that happened to
you after lunch.

SEBASTIAN (*distracted*). What? – Yes. That. But I'd expected
it. Conny hadn't given me any hope. He hasn't, really, for
the last three months.

MARK. Who else has she seen?

SEBASTIAN. The best in the country. She doesn't know it, of
course, but every man who looks her over in that hospital is
hand-picked. Of course they're casual with her, and don't
give their names. But they've all been by courtesy of my
kind Sunday paper – and all top boys on this disease.

MARK. There's no cure?

SEBASTIAN. There's this man in Denver, Colorado, who boasts a seventy per cent rate. But he's cagey. He won't take a case as advanced as this –

MARK. How do you know?

SEBASTIAN. I've asked him. I gave him all the facts and figures on the telephone, and got our medical correspondent to talk to him, too. No go, Mark. He won't take her, she's too far gone.

Bitterly.

He might spoil his record.

MARK. Isn't there anyone else?

SEBASTIAN. Faith healers galore, and acupuncture hounds. All phoneys. Christ, Mark, I haven't lacked for advice. If there'd been the faintest chance I'd have taken her to Timbuctoo – and told her I was covering Saharan literature. I'd already got my story ready for Denver. I'd induced some wretched little local college to offer me a resident lectureship. Jesus, imagine that! . . . Now, Winnie Slobberwicz, stop groping your neighbour and listen. Balls-ache, as you are pleased to pronounce him, is the name of an important French writer and not an occupational disease – You've seen her alone – Does she have the faintest suspicion I'm concealing something from her?

MARK. No.

SEBASTIAN. Swear?

MARK. Swear.

SEBASTIAN. I'm good about never remembering when she's been to the doctor, getting his name wrong and never noticing when she's feeling ill. Also never on any account saying: 'Look I'll do that, darling. Don't you bother.' Can you imagine anything giving the show away quicker than that?

MARK. Frankly, I can't.

SEBASTIAN. Yes. Being what we both agreed God made me does have its advantages when one's dealing with a dying wife.

He takes the report that he has shown MARK *from wherever it has been placed and glances at it.*

I suppose I'd better put this with the others.

MARK. Other what?

SEBASTIAN. Other reports – all of them.

He wheels out some library steps and places them beside a certain point at the book-shelves: in fact just below the hat-box.

Say: 'Hullo Lydia' very loudly if you see her on the stairs.

He makes an extension to the library steps, an operation which appears to need some application.

Yes. Uncle Conny sends me her reports every month. They vary so much you see. This is a disease that seems to go up and down. – Not steadily down like some. A little bit up one month, and one got hope. Then down next month. More down than the last down, and then one lost hope.

He flourishes the last report, and begins his ascent towards the hat-box.

MARK. Why do you keep a hat-box up there?

SEBASTIAN. To keep a hat in, you clot. What else?

He opens the box, takes out a top hat, puts his hand into the hat, removes a sheaf of papers, and then puts the hat on.

Topper to go to the Palace in for that OBE thing.

MARK. Jesus! Why did you keep those there?

SEBASTIAN. Security. Couldn't keep them at the office. Too many nosey parkers –

He clips the last report on to the bundle of papers, takes off the hat and shoves the hat and papers into the box.

MARK. That's ingenious.

SEBASTIAN. Yes. I got the idea from Edgar Allan Poe.

MARK. But wouldn't a drawer with a lock be safer?

SEBASTIAN. I haven't got one – but if I had she'd pick it.
Pries into everything, you know. Got her nose into my notes
for the new novel yesterday, after I'd carefully hidden them
in Gibbon's *Decline and Fall.*

Descending.

Dusting, she said. As if anyone would dust Gibbon without
criminal intent.

MARK. Mightn't she want to dust up there?

SEBASTIAN. Aha! Without these steps she *can't* dust up
there, and I'm the only one who knows how to elongate this
contraption –

*He shoves the extension back. He has spoken the truth:
without the elongation* LYDIA *would have no hope of
reaching it.*

Even Mrs MacReedy who is a giantess – if she's the Mrs
MacReedy I think she is – can only just flick it with the
very last feather of her duster.

Pleased with himself.

Yes. I wasn't in intelligence for nothing, you know.

He wheels the steps away, and then comes back to join
MARK. *He looks up at the box.*

No point, of course, in keeping anything more now. Not
after this biopsy –

MARK. Sebastian, are you quite sure you shouldn't tell her?

SEBASTIAN. Quite sure. For six long years she had nothing
to think of, Mark, except the almost certain prospect of
facing death, in one of a hundred really horrible ways . . .
To the Nazis the Balts were 'Untermenschen'. They didn't
deserve gas chambers. That was a luxury kept for the lucky
inmates of Auschwitz and Buchenwald down south – A three
star death compared to the 'Untermenschen' up north –

He sits down hurriedly, and drinks.

I send her up a bit for her refugee stories, but you know she
doesn't really tell them – not about herself –

He has his empty glass stretched out. MARK *takes it automatically.*

Oh, thanks so much . . . No. Up north it was open graves, and machine guns – Not always enough machine guns, so people got buried alive. That didn't matter to the Gauleiter, so long as he could report them dead.

MARK *comes back with his drink.*

Thanks. Lydia *was* reported dead, you know. That's how she managed to stay alive. When the Russians came back she was officially a non-person. Labour Camp material, perhaps, but not worth killing. And you know how she became a non-person? Did she ever tell you?

MARK. No.

SEBASTIAN. No, she wouldn't. She only told me once – one night in Bentinck Strasse – Well the drill was, they'd take them out at dusk into the open country, about a thousand at a time. And then they'd be made to dig this big ditch. It had to be pretty big to take a thousand bodies. Of course, they knew what it was for. No 'You're all going to the baths to be de-loused,' as in the gas-chambers. No. The 'Untermenschen' knew what they were digging.

He drinks.

Well, when that was finished to the Commandant's satisfaction they were divided into groups of about a hundred and stripped naked – gold fillings were pulled out, of course . . . That didn't apply to Lydia, who was only eighteen.

He takes another drink.

Then floodlights were turned on and each group was lined up facing the ditch and machine-gunned into the ditch . . . There were two gunners at either end of the ditch who sprayed the ones who seemed still to be alive – Then the next lot were lined up . . . Lydia's group was nearly the last – She'd seen the others die so she also saw how the machine-gunners operated . . . She counted the time-lag between the order to fire and the actual firing – half a second . . . At eighteen she was a – she was a very good swimmer, you

see – I mean, almost Olympic class, I gather – She was
trained to the starting gun. She heard the order 'fire,' and
dived into that ditch and landed without a scratch . . .
'Beating the gun' she called it . . . And she crawled under
the bodies of her friends, dead or dying, so that the two
gunners who both shot at her from each side missed her –
maybe killed some of those on top of her . . . Later the
bull-dozer shovelled the earth on top of the grave, and she
lay buried for two hours until she thought it was safe to
claw her way through the bodies and the earth into the
air . . . Although how she knew it was two hours, without a
watch, I'll always question . . . She says she counted second
by second, which is possible, I suppose . . . But how did she
survive that Baltic winter night, in the forest, naked? . . .
Well she did, and a farmer took her in, at risk to his own
life, in the morning – and gave her boy's clothes – his son's,
I think – and a lift to Tallinn, and a new life – until the
Russians came back. But that's another story.

He gets up himself to pour another drink. MARK *watches
him, concerned.*

No, Mark, I don't think it would be quite – the thing – do
you – to tell a lady who survived that kind of nonsense that
she's now dying of some bloody silly disease that's been
caused by her, as a teenager, not eating enough Kellogg's K
with her breakfast. Don't you think I'm right?

Pause.

MARK. Yeh. I think you might be right . . .

SEBASTIAN (*resuming his seat*). Another thing, Mark. If she
had the slightest inkling about herself, she'd worry herself
sick over Joey.

MARK. Not over you?

SEBASTIAN. Over *me?* Why should she worry herself over
me? She knows I can look after myself –

MARK. Does she?

SEBASTIAN. Well what with Mrs MacReedy and maybe
Prunella –

MARK. Isn't it just Mrs Reedy?

SEBASTIAN. It may well be Mrs Cholmondeley-Johnson-Smythe. Would you kindly not interfere in matters that are no concern of yours?

MARK. I'm sorry.

Pause.

About this lady Prunella – didn't you say yesterday that you couldn't bear –

SEBASTIAN. I know exactly what I said yesterday. Again it is no possible concern of yours –

MARK *goes to get himself another drink.*

The Bourbon is on the right, and, what with last night, you have come bloody close to drinking it flat.

MARK (*belligerently*). This is *my* Bourbon. Lydia bought it for *me* –

SEBASTIAN (*suddenly close to tears*). And you've left nothing for her favourite charity – 'The Little Sisters of the Poor.'

His back to MARK, *he believes he has concealed his emotion, but he hasn't.*

MARK (*at the drink table*). This Prunella –

SEBASTIAN. Yes?

MARK. I guess she means a bit more to you than you let on last night –

SEBASTIAN (*speaking with difficulty*). Why do you guess that?

MARK. Well, it wasn't so difficult. Jesus, did you play that up for Lydia!

SEBASTIAN. Was it so obvious?

MARK (*hastily*). Lydia didn't get it.

SEBASTIAN. Sure?

MARK. Certain.

SEBASTIAN. Terrible if she had. Yes, Prunella means a bit,
I suppose –

MARK. Enough for you to go to her and tell her this afternoon
that you'd got a letter from Lydia's doctor.

Pause.

SEBASTIAN. Yes. Enough for that.

MARK. Enough for her to make you forget that your son had a
television play on tonight at seven thirty.

SEBASTIAN. She didn't make me forget it. If she'd known
about it she'd have forced me to be here for it – Prunella's
all right, Mark – She's no Lydia, but she's all right –

Fumbling with a handkerchief.

No Lydia –

He begins to cry.

You've got to put up with this a bit, I'm afraid . . . Self-pity,
of course . . . You see the thing is, Mark – the *un*-crying,
unsentimental, un-self-pitying thing is that I didn't begin
really to love her until I knew I was losing her.

MARK (*not indulging him*). Yeh. That happens.

SEBASTIAN. Perhaps more to people like me than to people
like you. You've always loved her, haven't you?

MARK. I guess so.

SEBASTIAN. While I – I've only had about six months. Anybody but me would have started twenty-eight years sooner.

He hands out his drink to be refilled. MARK *takes it.*
Murmuring.

No Lydia –

'She'll come no more.
Never, never, never, never, never.'

Oh damn and blast. I'll never review that bloody man
Shakespeare again. I won't review anyone. After all they

all make you blub somewhere – if they're good enough.
No. I'll write my own blub stuff – that's what I'll do –

MARK. Good idea –

SEBASTIAN. All right. I may not sell the film rights for ten
million in advance, like some people –

MARK. Only one million – well, a million and a half – for the
new one, but who's counting?

SEBASTIAN. And I may not build palaces from its profits
in Eaton Square – East Seventy-eighth Street – Beverly
Drive – Tonga –

MARK (*affronted*). I haven't got a palace in Tonga –

SEBASTIAN. You will have. No. I will write the second
masterpiece of the twentieth century –

MARK. Which was the first?

SEBASTIAN. Modesty forbids. And you and your pathetic
attempt to steal Lydia will be in it –

MARK. Can't you find a better theme than that?

SEBASTIAN. Oh, you're not the theme. You're just a fringe
character – Not as you are, of course. No one would believe
that –

MARK. And Lydia?

SEBASTIAN. Oh no. No, not Lydia. I couldn't write Lydia,
and never will. Idiot!

MARK. Well, then, Joey?

SEBASTIAN (*suddenly still*). Yes, Joey, I suppose. Little
Liberal Joey. The new assenting young.

*Suddenly overcome again. The influx of adrenalin about his
new novel hasn't been quite enough.*

Poor little bastard! – Oh, the poor little sod – He worships
his mother – Too much for his psychological balances,
I suppose, but you can't quite blame him, can you?

MARK. No.

SEBASTIAN. And she thought he could put up with me for
    ten days?

MARK. She's an optimistic girl.

SEBASTIAN. Yes. Well tonight won't have helped her
    optimism . . . Poor little bugger . . . ten days without her.
    I don't like to think of that much.

MARK. Then come too.

SEBASTIAN. No. I could – but I've got to get used to – try to
    get used to – oh damn! Did I feel about her like this from
    the beginning? It's possible. It's possible. And wouldn't
    allow myself to? Yes, possible.

    Angrily.

    Do you know what 'le vice Anglais?' – the English vice –
    really is? Not flagellation, not pederasty – whatever the
    French believe it to be. It's our refusal to admit to our
    emotions. We think they demean us, I suppose.

    He covers his face.

    Well I'm being punished now, all right – for a lifetime of
    vice. Very moral ending to a Victorian novel. I'm becoming
    maudlin. But, oh Mark, life without Lydia will be such
    unending misery.

    He sees LYDIA *coming down the stairs.* SEBASTIAN
    *jumps up from his chair and turns his back, adroitly
    transforming emotion into huffiness.* LYDIA *looks at his
    back a long time. When* SEBASTIAN *turns to face her he is
    apparently dry-eyed, and holding his jaw as if in pain.*

SEBASTIAN (*with dignity*). Husband-beater!

LYDIA. I came to say I was sorry.

SEBASTIAN. I shall so inform my solicitors. Good night Mark.

MARK. Oh, am I going?

SEBASTIAN. No, I am.

    He directs another withering glance at LYDIA, *rubs his
    cheek and walks towards his work-room, even contriving a
    limp as he does so.*

LYDIA. Are you going to work? Isn't it too late?

SEBASTIAN. Yes, to the first. No, to the second.

LYDIA. Wouldn't you like some of this food?

SEBASTIAN. It would turn to ashes in my mouth.

He goes out.

LYDIA. Did I hurt him?

MARK. Not enough.

LYDIA. I could have hit him much harder, you know. And
kicked him too – on the ground. Queensberry Rules my
fanny. Is he really working or just sulking?

MARK. Sulking, I'd say. I'm going.

LYDIA (*looking anxiously at* SEBASTIAN*'s door*). Yes, I suppose you'd better.

She kisses him.

Thank you so very much, Marcus. He really did appreciate
it.

MARK. How is Joey?

LYDIA. He's bad, of course.

Angrily, at the door.

How could any human being do a thing like that to his son?
How *could* he? What's his excuse?

MARK. He forgot.

LYDIA. I mean his excuse for forgetting?

Pause.

MARK. About the best a man could have, I guess.

LYDIA (*amazed*). You take his side.

MARK. Yes, on this.

LYDIA. Well what *is* his excuse?

MARK. Good night, Lydia.

He goes to the door, leaving LYDIA *looking bewildered. Turning.*

Oh Christ! Has anybody ever been in such a spot? Look –

He points to the hat-box.

That thing up there. It needs dusting.

LYDIA. The hat-box?

MARK. Yes. You can see the dust from here.

LYDIA. But I can't reach it.

MARK *points to some library steps.* LYDIA, *utterly bewildered, goes to get them.* MARK *takes them from her, and wheels them into place. Then, with intense concentration, he works on the process of elongating them which he has plainly learned from watching* SEBASTIAN. *He finds the catch and pulls them up the necessary extra two or three feet.*

MARK. No. Not now. Tomorrow – when Sebastian's out. After you've dusted it – inside as well as out – you'll just have to play it your way – both of you. And then together or separately – tell me how *I'm* to play mine.

He restores the steps to their unextended length and puts them away.

LYDIA. I see. He's hidden something there.

MARK. Yes.

LYDIA. Something he doesn't want me to see.

MARK. You bet.

LYDIA. The wily bastard. Love letters?

MARK. Kind of.

LYDIA (*aghast*). You mean – serious?

MARK. Very serious, I think.

LYDIA. Larkin – I suppose –

MARK. No. Someone else.

LYDIA. Jesus – I wish I *had* kicked him. I wish I'd *killed* him.

Suddenly loyal.

And why are you giving him away? You're supposed to be his friend.

MARK. I'm supposed to be yours, too. That's what made my life, these last two days, a little confusing. Call you tomorrow.

He goes out. LYDIA, muttering imprecations, first looks at the hat-box, then firmly decides to resist the temptation. She comes into the sitting-room and sits down demurely. Then she looks at the hat-box again, and the library steps. Then she gets up cautiously and listens at SEBASTIAN's door. She hears him typing, and so do we. She darts to the library steps, rolls them into the hall and pulls down the hat-box, opening it and groping inside. Her fingers find what they are looking for and remove a pile of documents. Hastily she replaces the lid, and puts the hat-box back, leaving the library steps where they are. Then she puts on her glasses and settles herself on to the sofa. She riffles through the papers. They are all of identical size, and have needed no more than a few glances. They are, after all, familiar.

After a moment or two her legs give way, and she has to fall back on to the sofa. She has opened her bag to fumble for a handkerchief when SEBASTIAN opens his door. It is the matter of a split second for an accomplished document-peeper to stuff the papers into her bag and close it. The budding tears are a different matter. She had to brush those away. And she is conscious too of the tell-tale library steps.

SEBASTIAN (*gloomily*). I've been trying to write him a letter you could shove under his door. But it's no good. My mandarin style gets in the way.

LYDIA. It would.

She gets up casually to drape herself somewhere near the hall, masking the library steps.

SEBASTIAN. I suppose I'd better see the little sod.

LYDIA. What little sod?

SEBASTIAN. Are there two in the flat? Where is he?

LYDIA. If you're referring to our son – Joseph Cruttwell, dramatist – he's in bed.

SEBASTIAN. Oh darling, do stop sniffling. You know how I hate it.

LYDIA. I wasn't sniffling.

SEBASTIAN. You were. I could hear you from in there.

A lie.

And those things under your eyes are tears, aren't they?

He peers from a distance.

I'm not coming in range. I think you should know I once hit a sub-editor and he was off-duty for a week. And he wasn't any smaller than you either. However, enough of that. About Joey. What's done is done, and can, by dint of my overwhelming charm, be undone. I shall speak to him personally.

LYDIA. I shouldn't rely on your overwhelming charm.

SEBASTIAN. Thank you.

LYDIA. I mean why not just let him see you once as you really are.

SEBASTIAN. I have no idea what that sibylline utterance is supposed to mean. I think I know a father's duty towards his son without prompting from you, Madam.

LYDIA. I think you do.

SEBASTIAN. I gather you tried to torture him tonight into staying with me, while you're off sunning yourself in Monte Carlo.

LYDIA. There was no torture involved. He *volunteered.* He said he'd be happy to do it.

SEBASTIAN. Christ, what an appalling liar you are, sometimes.

LYDIA. I'm not a liar! I'm just –

She stops.

SEBASTIAN. What?

LYDIA. An optimist.

SEBASTIAN. Isn't that a liar?

LYDIA. Not necessarily. He'd like to stay with you here for ten days.

Pause.

SEBASTIAN. After tonight?

LYDIA (*bravely*). Why not?

Pause.

SEBASTIAN. Why are you leaning there like Madame Récamier?

LYDIA. I've been putting books in their right places, under your orders, sir.

SEBASTIAN. Good. That'll be a change. All right. Go and get the little bugger down.

LYDIA. No.

SEBASTIAN. No?

LYDIA. You go up.

SEBASTIAN (*outraged*). Go up? Knock timidly at his door and beg leave to enter that room with all those Liberal posters on the wall – crawl across the carpet like a penitent, abase myself like Henry IV at Canossa, scourge myself – all right, I'll go up.

He goes to the stairs, climbing reluctantly.

Why are you looking at me like that?

LYDIA. A cat may look at a King.

SEBASTIAN. Are you pissed again?

LYDIA. Oh yes.

SEBASTIAN. Vodka.

LYDIA. Something – kind of – headier –

SEBASTIAN. Kirsch, or slivovitz or something? My God, darling, you'll end up in an alcoholics' ward.

He disappears. Immediately LYDIA *darts into the hall climbs the steps and deposits the papers inside. She has just wheeled the steps back when* SEBASTIAN *reappears.*

I looked in and the little bastard was asleep.

Relieved.

Tomorrow, don't you think?

He scoops some food on to a plate. Plying a fork.

Hm. This is rather good. Who made it? Joey?

LYDIA, *free now to move, pulls her right fist back.*

Oh *you* did?

LYDIA. It's my crab mousse, and you've had it a million times.

SEBASTIAN. It just seemed better than usual.

JOEY, *in a dressing-gown, is coming downstairs. Both parents watch him as he walks in a dignified manner past his father, cutting him dead, and up to* LYDIA.

JOEY. I'm very sorry, Mum. I left you to clear up alone.

LYDIA. Oh that's all right, darling. I can do that myself.

JOEY. I'll help you.

He picks up two dishes and carries them up to the kitchen. SEBASTIAN *exchanges a meaning glance with* LYDIA.

SEBASTIAN (*loudly*). Darling, would you fix that draught for me in there.

LYDIA. Oh, yes, I will.

JOEY reappears, still walking with dignity.

SEBASTIAN. I think it's coming from the window.

LYDIA. Yes. I shouldn't be surprised.

She goes in to the work-room.

SEBASTIAN. Joey, put those things down.

JOEY, at first, is inclined to disobey. SEBASTIAN *takes them from him.*

Anyway I'm eating from this one.

JOEY. I'm very sorry. If I'd known I wouldn't have touched it.

SEBASTIAN. You've a perfect right to be as rude to me as you like, and to call me every name you can think of. Tonight I behaved to you as badly as any father has ever behaved to his son. If my father had done that to me when I was your age I'd have walked straight out of his house and never talked to him again.

JOEY. You did, didn't you?

SEBASTIAN. No. I was turned out. I may have told you I walked out, because it sounds better. In fact I was booted. A little trouble with one of the maids. I can only say, Joey, that tonight I behaved like a thoughtless bastard – that's the word your Mum used. To Mark I said 'shit' – 'an uncaring shit' and meant it. I am that, sometimes, and I behave like that sometimes. If you like you can say usually. Or even always. It may be true. But tonight was the worst thing I've ever done to anyone, anywhere. I may do some bad things to you, Joey, in the future – if we're still seeing each other – but one thing you must know – I can't ever do anything quite as bad as I did tonight. Not even I can break the world record twice –

JOEY. I don't believe you forgot. I believe you did it deliberately.

SEBASTIAN. I can see you'd rather think that. So would I. It's less damaging to the ego. The plain, sordid fact is that I forgot.

JOEY. How could you, Dad?

SEBASTIAN. I did. And I have no excuse at all. Now listen. What I intend to do is this. I shall get our television man to ask to have it re-run –

JOEY. Oh Dad – this is all talk.

SEBASTIAN. At Television Centre, for me, for him – not for my Editor who's in Tangier – and for anyone else who wants to see it. You, of course, too. And our television critic will review it. I don't know what he'll say, and it'll have to be next week, but he'll mention it in his column, I promise.

JOEY. Is this on the level, or will you forget again?

SEBASTIAN. I said you could insult me, but there's no need to kick me in the crutch. Now if I do that for you will you do something for me?

JOEY (*suspiciously*). What?

SEBASTIAN. Sit in that chair.

He forces him into one and then brings over the chess table.

And show me for once how you can justify all that hissing that goes on behind my chair.

JOEY. Dad, it's late.

SEBASTIAN. Only for Liberals. Not for men. Go on. You be white. Fifty pence on it?

JOEY. I'll want a two pawns' handicap.

SEBASTIAN. One.

JOEY. Done.

SEBASTIAN takes one of his pawns off. JOEY moves. SEBASTIAN moves. JOEY moves.

SEBASTIAN. That's not in *my* 'Twelve Easy Openings for Beginners'.

SEBASTIAN moves. JOEY thinks. LYDIA, who has plainly had her ear glued to the keyhole, slips out of the work-room. She watches them for a second. JOEY moves. SEBASTIAN moves.

JOEY (*rising*). Right. My game.

SEBASTIAN. What do you mean your game?

JOEY. You moved your King three squares.

SEBASTIAN. I beg your pardon, my Queen.

Horrified.

My *King?* Oh blast and bugger that Mark Walters! These pieces are going, straight back to Hong-Kong. I told him a hundred times –

He is putting the pieces back on the board again. JOEY *has stood up.*

JOEY. Fifty pence, please.

SEBASTIAN. Are you mad, boy?

JOEY. The rules say firmly –

LYDIA. You must play the rules, dear.

SEBASTIAN. You keep out of this! Go and do something useful somewhere. Better still, go to bed.

JOEY. Yes, Mum. We'll clear up.

SEBASTIAN. Yes, Joey will clear up.

LYDIA. Give Joey his fifty pence.

SEBASTIAN. Oh bugger you both!

He forks up.

LYDIA. Charming loser, isn't he?

SEBASTIAN. Loser my arse! I didn't lose. I made a tiny human error in laying out these monstrosities of chessmen –

JOEY *is going.* SEBASTIAN *catches his sleeve.*

Oh, my boy. Oh no. If you think you're taking that fifty pence of mine to bed, you're making a big mistake. All right. Start again. Double or quits. Same moves, but this time with the right pieces in the right places –

They move rapidly in silence. LYDIA *watches them for a moment, putting her arm lightly on* SEBASTIAN*'s shoulder.*

LYDIA. Well, good night.

JOEY *jumps up to kiss his mother.*

SEBASTIAN (*irritated*). Don't do that. It upsets concentration. You could have kissed her sitting down, couldn't you?

He does exactly that, slapping her playfully on the behind. She goes to the stairs. SEBASTIAN *concentrates on the board. To* JOEY.

I'm afraid your Liberal Party Headquarters is coming under a little pressure.

JOEY. Your Kremlin doesn't look too happy either, Dad.

LYDIA *turns to look back at them.*

SEBASTIAN (*to* JOEY). Yes, I can see you have played before. Well, well, well. Do you know those ten days without her might be quite fun –

He looks up casually. If we didn't know his secret we might even believe him when he says:

Oh sorry, darling. Didn't see you were still there.

LYDIA *smiles. In fact, radiantly.*

LYDIA. I know you didn't.

SEBASTIAN. Go on. Move, Joey.

She goes on slowly up the stairs.

We haven't got all night ahead of us.

LYDIA. *disappears from sight.*

Except, I suppose, we have.

Curtain.